INDIA AND THE WORLD

INDIA AND THE WORLD

Essays

JAWAHARLAL NEHRU

GYAN

Published by

GYAN

Gyan Publishing House
5, Ansari Road
Daryaganj, New Delhi-110002
Phone: 011-47034999, 9811692060
E-mail: books@gyanbooks.com

Distribution Network
gyanbooks.com
India, USA, Canada, UK, Australia

ISBN: 978-93-7169-048-5 (PB)

First Published, 1936

2nd Impression 2025

Printed at: Gyan Press, Delhi.

INDIA AND THE WORLD
Author: JAWAHARLAL NEHRU

INDIA AND THE WORLD

INDIA AND THE WORLD

Essays

by

JAWAHARLAL NEHRU

EDITOR'S PREFACE

EDITOR'S PREFACE

FOR several years past attempts have been made to publish some of Mr. Jawaharlal Nehru's writings in this country, but a number of difficulties have prevented this until now. Mr. Nehru's visit to Europe at the end of 1935, to spend what proved to be the last months of her life by the bedside of his wife, has at last led to the fulfilment of this desire. His *Autobiography* has already appeared, and has been very well received, and his *Glimpses of World History*, written as letters to his schoolgirl daughter while he was in prison, is likely to be published in an English edition very soon. There seemed to be a need, also, that some of Mr. Nehru's writings on politics, especially some of the most recent, should be available for Western readers in a handy and permanent form. Hence this volume.

For the immediate future of Britain, and her place in the world, few things can be more important than a first-hand knowledge of the chief men and women in Indian public life. The present ignorance of every other important Indian is as serious as the misunderstanding of the one whose name is known—Mahatma Gandhi. Nor is it enough to read Press reports—often coloured or distorted—of what Indian leaders say and do. We must go to the source.

Mr. Nehru is one of those Indians who constantly sees his own country not as an end in itself, but as part of the world, influenced by world forces. Thus, in the first three essays that follow—two of them being Mr.

Nehru's presidential addresses to the National Congress, in 1929 and 1936, the other his reflections on tendencies in India in 1933—although he is addressing himself to Indians, and is giving attention to a number of internal problems, the reader will find that even these domestic issues are again and again related to world tendencies.

Then follow some shorter essays written in prison between 1933 and 1935, concerning various matters and illustrating various moods. The later part of the book contains essays and other writings of the present year, while Mr. Nehru was in Europe. Perhaps one peculiar value of these latest writings is that we are given an opportunity to see ourselves through Indian eyes. Many books are published to give English views of India and the East; too few to give Indian views of England and the West. For this reason the editor was strongly disposed to put the "Letter to an Englishman" last. But from what he knows of Mr. Nehru, he believes it is juster to him to conclude, not with the crimes of England, but with the needs of the Indian peasants: for he suspects that the Indian peasant has a much larger place in Mr. Nehru's mind than the British Government. So we take leave of him, after he has overthrown the British Raj, reconstructing the Indian village.

Mr. Nehru left to the present writer the somewhat embarrassing task of selecting the material for this book, and of preparing it for the press. It is to be remembered that some of these writings have been produced under the pressure of much activity, in response to various urgent requests—they were not written with a view to subsequent collected publication. Consequently, there is some overlapping. Certain writings have been omitted altogether to avoid undue repetition; for the rest, avoidance of all repetition could only have been achieved by more cutting and editing than seemed proper. The reader will not, I believe, find it excessive. One or two friends who prefer anonymity have given valuable advice; but the editor is alone responsible for the final selection and the footnotes.

Acknowledgments are due to Messrs. Kitabistan, of Allahabad, the *Modern Review* of Calcutta, *L'Europe* and *Vendredi* of Paris, *Time and Tide*, and the *Socialist*, for reproduction of matter first published by them.

H. G. A.

May 1936

CONTENTS

I

PRESIDENTIAL ADDRESS TO THE NATIONAL CONGRESS, LAHORE, DECEMBER, 1929

FOR four-and-forty years this National Congress has laboured for the freedom of India. During this period it has somewhat slowly but surely awakened national consciousness from its long stupor and built up the national movement. If to-day we are gathered here at a crisis of our destiny, conscious of our strength as well as of our weakness, and looking with hope and apprehension to the future, it is well that we give first thought to those who spent their lives with little hope of reward so that those that follow them may have the joy of achievement. Many of the giants of old are not with us and we of a later day, standing on an eminence of their creation, may often decry their efforts. That is the way of the world. But none of you can forget them or the great work they did in laying the foundations of a free India. And none of us can ever forget that glorious band of men and women who, without recking the consequences, have laid down their young lives or spent their bright youth in suffering and torment in utter protest against a foreign domination. Many of their names even are not known to us. They laboured and suffered in silence without any expectation of public applause, and by their heart's blood they nursed the tender plant of India's freedom. While many of us temporized and compromised, they stood up and proclaimed a people's right to freedom and declared to the world that India, even in her degradation, had the spark of life in her, because she refused to submit to tyranny and serfdom. Brick by brick has our national movement been built up, and often on the prostrate bodies of her martyred sons has India advanced. The giants of old may not be with us, but the courage of old is with us still, and India can yet produce martyrs like Jatindas and Wizaya.

This is the glorious legacy that we have inherited, and you wish to put me in charge of it! I know well that I occupy this honoured place by chance more than by your deliberate design. Your desire was to choose another—one who towers above all others in this present-day world of ours—and there could have been no wiser choice. But fate and he conspired together and thrust me against your will and mine into this terrible seat of responsibility. Should I express my gratitude to you for having placed me in this dilemma? But I am grateful indeed for your confidence in one who strangely lacks it himself.

You will discuss many vital national problems that face us to-day, and your decisions may change the course of Indian history. But you are not the only people that are faced with problems. The whole world to-day is one vast question mark, and every country and every people is in the melting-pot. The age of faith, with the comfort and stability it brings, is past, and there is questioning about everything, however permanent or sacred it might have appeared to our forefathers. Everywhere there is doubt and restlessness, and the foundations of the State and society are in process of transformation. Old-established ideas of liberty, justice, property, and even the family are being attacked, and the outcome hangs in the balance. We appear to be in a dissolving period of history, when the world is in labour and out of her travail will give birth to a new order.

No one can say what the future will bring, but we may assert with some confidence that Asia, and even India, will play a determining part in future world policy. The brief day of European domination is already approaching its end. Europe has ceased to be the centre of activity and interest. The future lies with America and Asia. Owing to false and incomplete history many of us have been led to think that Europe has always dominated over the rest of the world, and Asia has always let the legions of the West thunder past and has plunged in thought again. We have forgotten that for millennia the legions of Asia overran Europe, and modern Europe itself largely consists of the descendants of these invaders from Asia. We have forgotten that it was India that finally broke the military power of Alexander. Thought has undoubtedly been the glory of Asia and specially of India, but in the field of action the record of Asia has been equally great. But none of us desires that the legions of Asia or Europe should overrun the continents again. We have all had enough of them.

India to-day is a part of a world movement. Not only China, Turkey, Persia, and Egypt, but also Russia and the countries of the West are taking part in this movement, and India cannot isolate herself from it. We have our own problems, difficult and intricate, and we cannot run away from them and take shelter in the wider problems that affect the world. But if we ignore the world we do so at our peril. Civilization to-day, such as it is, is not the creation of the monopoly of one people or nation. It is a composite fabric to which all countries have contributed and then have adapted to suit their particular needs. And if India has a message to give to the world, as I hope she has, she has also to receive and learn much from the messages of other peoples.

When everything is changing it is well to remember the long course of Indian history. Few things in history are more amazing than the wonderful stability of the social structure in India which withstood the impact of numerous alien influences and thousands of years of change and conflict. It withstood them because it always sought to absorb them and tolerate them. Its aim was not to exterminate but to establish an equilibrium between different cultures. Aryans and non-Aryans settled down together recognizing each other's right to their culture, and outsiders who came, like the Parsis, found a welcome and a place in the social order. With the coming of the Moslems the equilibrium was disturbed, but India sought to restore it, and largely succeeded. Unhappily for us, before we could adjust our differences, the political structure broke down, the British came and we fell.

Great as was the success of India in evolving a stable society she failed in a vital particular, and because she failed in this, she fell and remains fallen. No solution was found for the problem of equality. India deliberately ignored this and built up her social structure on inequality, and we have the tragic consequences of this policy in the millions of our people who till yesterday were suppressed and had little opportunity for growth

When Europe fought her wars of religion and Christians massacred each other in the name of their Saviour, India was tolerant, although, alas, there is little of this toleration to-day. Having attained some measure of religious liberty, Europe sought after political liberty and political and legal equality. Having attained these also she finds that they mean very little without economic liberty and equality. And so to-day politics have ceased to have much meaning, and the most vital question is that of social and economic equality.

India also will have to find a solution to this problem, and until she does so her political and social structure cannot have stability. That solution need not necessarily follow the example of any other country. It must, if it has to endure, be based on the genius of her people and be an outcome of her thought and culture. And when it is found, the unhappy differences between various communities, which trouble us to-day and keep back our freedom, will automatically disappear.

Indeed the real differences have already largely gone, but fear of each other and distrust and suspicion remain and sow seeds of discord. The problem before us is not one of removing differences. They can well remain side by side and enrich our many-sided culture. The problem is how to remove fear and suspicion, and, being intangible, they are hard to get at. An earnest attempt was made to do so last year by the All Parties Committee, and much progress was made towards the goal. But we must admit with sorrow that success has not wholly crowned its efforts. Many of our Muslim and Sikh friends have strenuously opposed the solutions suggested, and passions have been roused over mathematical figures and percentages. Logic and cold reason are poor weapons to fight fear and distrust. Only faith and generosity can overcome them. I can only hope that the leaders of various communities will have this faith and generosity in ample measure. What shall we gain for ourselves or for our community if all of us are slaves in a slave country? And what can we lose if once we remove the shackles from India and can breathe the air of freedom again? Do we want outsiders, who are not of us and who have kept us in bondage, to be the protectors of our little rights and privileges, when they deny us the very right to freedom? No majority can crush a determined minority, and no minority can be sufficiently protected by a little addition to its seats in a legislature. Let us remember that in the world to-day, almost everywhere, a very small minority holds wealth and power and dominates over the great majority.

I have no love for bigotry and dogmatism in religion, and I am glad that they are weakening. Nor do I love communalism in any shape or form. I find it difficult to appreciate why political or economic rights should depend on the membership of a religious group or community. I can fully understand the right to freedom in religion and the right to one's culture, and in India specially, which has always acknowledged and granted these rights, it should be no difficult matter to ensure their continuance. We have only to find out some way whereby we may root out the fear and distrust that darken our horizon to-day. The politics of a subject race are largely based on fear and hatred, and we have been too long under subjection to get rid of them easily.

I was born a Hindu, but I do not know how far I am justified in calling myself one or in speaking on behalf of Hindus. But birth still counts in this country, and by right of birth I shall venture to submit to the leaders of the Hindus that it should be their privilege to take the lead in generosity. Generosity is not only good morals, but is often good politics and sound expediency. And it is inconceivable to me that in a free India the Hindus can ever be powerless. So far as I am concerned I would gladly ask our Muslim and Sikh friends to take what they will without protest or argument from me. I know that the time is coming soon when these labels and appellations will have little meaning and when our struggles will be on an economic basis. Meanwhile it matters little what our mutual arrangements are, provided only that we do not build up barriers which will come in the way of future progress.

The time has indeed already come when the All-Parties Report has to be put aside and we march forward unfettered to our goal. You will remember the resolution of the last Congress which fixed a year of grace for the adoption of the All-Parties scheme.* That year is nearly over, and the natural issue of that decision is for this Congress to declare in favour of independence and devise sanctions to achieve it.

That year has not brought Dominion Status or the All-Parties Constitution. It has brought instead suffering and greater repression of our national and labour movements, and how many of our comrades are to-day forcibly kept away from us by the alien power! How many of them suffer exile in foreign countries and are refused facilities to return to their motherland! The army of occupation holds our country in its iron grip, and the whip of the master is ever ready to come down on the best of us who dare to raise their heads. The answer to the Calcutta resolution has been clear and definite.

Recently there has been a seeming offer of peace.

* A committee representing all the important political parties and groups in India prepared a "Dominion Status" Constitution for India. The National Congress decided in 1928 at Calcutta that unless the British Government accepted this scheme within one year, it would revert to its demand for complete independence, and undertake a campaign to secure it.

The Viceroy has stated on behalf of the British Government that the leaders of Indian opinion will be invited to confer with the Government on the subject of India's future constitution. The Viceroy meant well and his language was the language of peace. But even a Viceroy's goodwill and courteous phrases are poor substitutes for the hard facts that confront us. We have sufficient experience of the devious ways of British diplomacy to beware of it. The offer that the British Government made was vague, and there was no commitment or promise of performance. Only by the greatest stretch of imagination could it be interpreted as a possible response to the Calcutta resolution. Many leaders of various political parties met together soon after and considered it. They gave it the most favourable interpretation, for they desired peace and were willing to go half-way to meet it. But in courteous language they made it clear what the vital conditions for its acceptance were. Many of us who believed in independence and were convinced that the offer was only a device to lead us astray and create division in our ranks, suffered bitter anguish and were torn with doubt. Were we justified in precipitating a terrible national struggle with all its inevitable consequences of suffering for many when there was even an outside chance of honourable peace? With much searching of heart we signed that manifesto, and I know not to-day if we did right or wrong. Later came the explanations and amplifications in the British Parliament and elsewhere, and all doubt, if doubt there were, was removed as to the true significance of the offer. Even so your Working Committee chose to keep open the door of negotiation and left it to this Congress to take the final decision.

During the last few days there has been another discussion of this subject in the British House of Commons, and the Secretary of State for India has endeavoured to point out that successive Governments have tried to prove, not only by words but by deeds also, the sincerity of their faith in regard to India. We must recognize Mr. Wedgwood Benn's desire to do something for India and his anxiety to secure the goodwill of the Indian people. But his speech and the other speeches made in Parliament carry us no further. "Dominion Status in action," to which he has drawn attention, has been a snare for us, and has certainly not reduced the exploitation of India. The burdens on the Indian masses are even greater to-day because of this "Dominion Status in action" and the so-called constitutional reforms of ten years ago. High Commissioners in London, and representatives on the League of Nations, and the purchase of stores, and Indian Governors and high officials are no parts of our demand. We want to put an end to the exploitation of India's poor and to get the reality of power and not merely the livery of office.

Mr. Wedgwood Benn has given us a record of the achievements of the past decade. He could have added to it by referring to Martial Law in the Punjab and the Jallianwala Bagh shooting and the repression and exploitation that have gone on continually during this period of "Dominion Status in action." He has given us some insight into what more of Dominion Status may mean for us. It will mean the shadow of authority to a handful of Indians, and more repression and exploitation of the masses.

What will this Congress do? The conditions for co-operation remain unfulfilled. Can we co-operate so long as there is no guarantee that real freedom will come to us? Can we co-operate when our comrades lie in prison and repression continues? Can we co-operate until we are assured that real peace is sought after and not merely a tactical advantage over us? Peace cannot come at the point of the bayonet, and if we are to continue to be dominated over by an alien people, let us at least be no consenting parties to it.

If the Calcutta resolution holds, we have but one goal to-day, that of independence. Independence is not a happy word in the world to-day, for it means exclusiveness and isolation. Civilization has had enough of narrow nationalism and gropes towards a wider co-operation and interdependence. And if we use the word independence we do so in no sense hostile to the larger ideal. Independence for us means complete freedom from British domination and British imperialism. Having attained our freedom I have no doubt that India will welcome all attempts at world co-operation and federation, and will even agree to give up part of her own independence to a larger group of which she is an equal member.

The British Empire to-day is not such a group, and cannot be so long as it dominates over millions of peoples and holds large areas of the world's surface despite the will of their inhabitants. It cannot be a true commonwealth so long as imperialism is its basis and the exploitation of other races its chief means of sustenance. The British Empire to-day is indeed gradually undergoing a process of political dissolution. It is in a state of unstable equilibrium. The Union of South Africa is not a very happy member of the family, nor is the Irish Free State a willing one. Egypt drifts away. India could never be an equal member of the Commonwealth unless imperialism and all it implies is discarded. So long as this is not done India's position in the Empire must be one of subservience, and her exploitation will continue. The embrace of the British Empire is a dangerous thing. It cannot be the life-giving embrace of affection freely given and returned. And if it is not that, it will be, what it has been in the past, the embrace of death.

There is talk of world peace and pacts have been signed by the nations of the world. But despite pacts armaments grow and beautiful language is the only homage that is paid to the goddess of peace. Peace can only come when the causes of war are removed. So long as there is the domination of one country over another, or the exploitation of one class by another, there will always be attempts to subvert the existing order, and no stable equilibrium can endure. Out of imperialism and capitalism peace can never come. And it is because the British Empire stands for these, and bases itself on the exploitation of the masses, that we can find no willing place in it. No gain that may come to us is worth anything unless it helps in removing the grievous burdens on our masses. The weight of a great empire is heavy to carry, and long our people have endured it. Their backs are bent and down and their spirit has almost broken. How will they share in the commonwealth partnership if the burden of exploitation continues? Many of the problems we have to face are the problems of vested interests, mostly created or encouraged by the British Government. The interests of rulers of Indian States, of British officials, and British capital and Indian capital, and of the owners of big zamindaris are ever thrust before us, and they clamour for protection. The unhappy millions who really need protection are almost voiceless, and have few advocates. So long as the British Empire continues in India, in whatever shape it may do so, it will strengthen these vested interests and create more. And each one of them will be a fresh obstacle in our way. Of necessity the Government has to rely on oppression, and the symbol of its rule is the secret service with its despicable and contemptible train of *agents provocateurs*, informers, and approvers.

We have had much controversy about independence and Dominion Status, and we have quarrelled about words. But the real thing is the conquest of power by whatever name it may be called. I do not think that any form of Dominion Status applicable to India will give us real power. A test of this power would be the entire withdrawal of the alien army of occcupation and economic control. Let us, therefore, concentrate on these and the rest will follow easily.

We stand, therefore, to-day for the fullest freedom of India. This Congress has not acknowledged and will not acknowledge the right of the British Parliament to dictate to us in any way. To it we make no appeal. But we do appeal to the parliament and conscience of the world, and to them we shall declare, I hope, that India submits no longer to any foreign domination. To-day or to-morrow we may not be strong enough to assert our will. We are very conscious of our weakness, and there is no boasting in us or pride of strength. But let no one, least of all England, mistake or underrate the meaning or strength of our resolve. Solemnly, with full knowledge of consequences, I hope, we shall take it and there will be no turning back. A great nation cannot be thwarted for long when once its mind is clear and resolved. If to-day we fail and to-morrow brings no success, the day after will follow and bring achievement.

We are weary of strife and hunger for peace and opportunity to work constructively for our country. Do we enjoy the breaking up of our homes and the sight of our brave young men going to prison or facing the halter? Does the worker like going on strike and losing even his miserable pittance and starving? He does so by sheer compulsion when there is no other way for him. And we who take this perilous path of national strife do so because there is no other way to an honourable peace. But we long for peace, and the hand of fellowship will always be stretched out to all who may care to grasp it. But behind the hand will be a body which will not bend to injustice, and a mind that will not surrender on any vital point.

With the struggle before us the time for determining our future constitution is not yet. For two years or more we have drawn up constitutions, and finally the All Parties Committee put a crown to these efforts by drawing up a scheme of its own which the Congress adopted for a year. The labour that went to the making of this scheme was not wasted, and India has profited by it. But the year is past and we have to face new circumstances which require action rather than constitution making. Yet we cannot ignore the problems that beset us and that will make or mar our struggle and our future constitution. We have to aim at social adjustment and equilibrium, and to overcome the forces of disruption that have been the bane of India.

I must frankly confess that I am a Socialist and a republican, and am no believer in kings and princes, or in the order which produces the modern kings of industry, who have greater power over the lives and fortunes of men than even the kings of old, and whose methods are as predatory as those of the old feudal aristocracy. I recognize, however, that it may not be possible for a body constituted as is this National Congress, and in the present circumstances of the country, to adopt a full Socialistic programme. But we must realize that the philosophy of Socialism has gradually permeated the entire structure of society the world over, and almost the only points in dispute are the pace and the methods of advance to its full realization. India will have to go that way, too, if she seeks to end her poverty and inequality, though she may evolve her own methods and may adapt the ideal to the genius of her race.

We have three major problems—the minorities, the Indian States, and labour and peasantry. I have dealt already with the question of minorities. I shall only repeat that we must give the fullest assurance by our words and deeds that their culture and traditions will be safe.

The Indian States, even for India, are the most curious relics of a bygone age. Many of their rulers apparently still believe in the divine right of kings—puppet kings though they be—and consider the State and all it contains to be their personal property, which they can squander at will. A few of them have a sense of responsibility and have endeavoured to serve their people, but many of them have hardly any redeeming feature. It is perhaps unjust to blame them, for they are but the products of a vicious system, and it is the system that will ultimately have to go. One of the rulers has told us frankly that even in case of war between India and England he will stand for England and fight against his mother country. That is the measure of his patriotism. It is not surprising, then, that they claim, and their claim finds acceptance with the British Government, that they alone can represent their subjects at any conference, and no one even of their subjects may have any say. The Indian States cannot live apart from the rest of India, and their rulers must, unless they accept their inevitable limitations, go the way of others who thought like them.

And the only people who have a right to determine the future of the States must be the people of those States, including the rulers. This Congress which claims self-determination cannot deny it to the people of the States. Meanwhile, the Congress is perfectly willing to confer with such rulers as are prepared to do so, and to devise means whereby the transition may not be too sudden. But in no event can the people of the States be ignored.

Our third major problem is the biggest of all. For India means the peasantry and labour, and to the extent that we raise them and satisfy their wants, will we succeed in our task. And the measure of the strength of our national movement will be the measure of their adherence to it. We can only gain them to our side by our espousing their cause, which is really the country's cause. The Congress has often expressed its goodwill toward them, but beyond that it has not gone. The Congress, it is said, must hold the balance fairly between capital and labour and zamindar and tenant. But the balance has been and is terribly weighted on one side, and to maintain the *status quo* is to maintain injustice and exploitation. The only way to right it is to do away with the domination of any one class over another. The All-India Congress Committee accepted this ideal of social and economic change in a resolution it passed some months ago in Bombay. I hope the Congress will also set its seal on it, and will further draw up a programme of such changes as can be immediately put in operation.

In this programme perhaps the Congress as a whole

cannot go very far to-day. But it must keep the ultimate ideal in view and work for it. The question is not one merely of wages and charity doled out by an employer or landlord. Paternalism in industry or in the land is but a form of charity with all its sting and its utter incapacity to root out the evil. The new theory of trusteeship, which some advocate, is equally barren. For trusteeship means that the power for good or evil remains with the self-appointed trustee, and he may exercise it as he will. The sole trusteeship that can be fair is the trusteeship of the nation and not of one individual or a group. Many Englishmen honestly consider themselves the trustees for India, and yet to what a condition have they reduced our country!

We have to decide for whose benefit industry must be run and the land produce food. To-day the abundance that the land produces is not for the peasant or the labourer who work on it; and industry's chief function is supposed to be to produce millionaires. However golden the harvest and heavy the dividends, the mud huts and hovels and nakedness of our people testify to the glory of the British Empire and of our present social system.

Our economic programme must, therefore, be based on a human outlook and must not sacrifice man to money. If an industry cannot be run without starving its workers, then the industry must close down. If the workers on the land have not enough to eat, then the intermediaries who deprive them of their full share must go. The least that every worker in field or factory is entitled to is a minimum wage which will enable him to live in moderate comfort, and humane hours of labour which do not break his strength and spirit. The All Parties Committee accepted the principle and included it in their recommendations. I hope the Congress will also do so, and will in addition be prepared to accept its natural consequences. Further, that it will adopt the well-known demands of labour for a better life, and will give every assistance to it to organize itself and prepare itself for the day when it can control industry on a co-operative basis.

But industrial labour is only a small part of India, although it is rapidly becoming a force that cannot be ignored. It is the peasantry that cry loudly and piteously for relief, and our programme must deal with their present condition. Real relief can only come by a great change in the land laws and the basis of the present system of land tenure. We have among us many big landowners, and we welcome them. But they must realize that the ownership of large estates by individuals, which is the outcome of a state resembling the old feudalism of Europe, is a rapidly disappearing phenomenon all over the world. Even in countries which are the strongholds of capitalism the large estates are being split up and given to the peasantry who work on them. In India also we have large areas where the system of peasant proprietorship prevails, and we shall have to extend this all over the country. I hope that in doing so we may have the co-operation of some at least of the big landowners.

It is not possible for this Congress at its annual session to draw up any detailed economic programme.

It can only lay down some general principles and call upon the All-India Congress Committee to fill in the details in co-operation with the representatives of the Trades Union Congress and other organizations which are vitally interested in this matter. Indeed I hope that the co-operation between this Congress and the Trades Union Congress will grow, and the two organizations will fight side by side in future struggles.

All these are pious hopes till we gain power, and the real problem, therefore, before us is the conquest of power. We shall not do so by subtle reasoning or argument or lawyers' quibbles, but by the forging of sanctions to enforce the nation's will. To that end this Congress must address itself.

The past year has been one of preparation for us, and we have made every effort to reorganize and strengthen the Congress organization. The results have been considerable, and our organization is in a better state to-day than at any time since the reaction which followed the non-co-operation movement. But our weaknesses are many and are apparent enough. Mutual strife, even within Congress committees, is unhappily too common and election squabbles drain all our strength and energy. How can we fight a great fight if we cannot get over this ancient weakness of ours and rise above our petty selves? I earnestly hope that with a strong programme of action before the country our perspective will improve and we will not tolerate this barren and demoralizing strife.

What can this programme be? Our choice is limited, not by our own constitution, which we can change at our will, but by facts and circumstances. Article I of our constitution lays down that our methods must be legitimate and peaceful. Legitimate I hope they will always be, for we must not sully the great cause for which we stand by any deed that will bring dishonour to it and that we may ourselves regret later. Peaceful I should like them to be, for the methods of peace are more desirable and more enduring than those of violence. Violence too often brings reaction and demoralization in its train, and in our country specially it may lead to disruption. It is perfectly true that organized violence rules the world to-day, and it may be that we could profit by its use. But we have not the material or the training for organized violence, and individual or sporadic violence is a confession of despair. The great majority of us, I take it, judge the issue not on moral but on practical grounds, and if we reject the way of violence it is because it promises no substantial results. But if this Congress or the nation at any future time comes to the conclusion that methods of violence will rid us of slavery then I have no doubt that it will adopt them. Violence is bad, but slavery is far worse. Let us also remember that the great apostle of non-violence has himself told us that it is better to fight than to refuse to fight out of cowardice.

Any great movement for liberation to-day must necessarily be a mass movement, and mass movements must essentially be peaceful, except in times of organized revolt. Whether we have the non-co-operation of a decade ago or the modern industrial weapon of the general strike, the basis is peaceful organization and peaceful action. And if the principal movement is a peaceful one contemporaneous attempts at sporadic violence can only distract attention and weaken it. It is not possible to carry on at one and the same time the two movements side by side. We have to choose and strictly to abide by our choice. What the choice of this Congress is likely to be I have no doubt. It can only choose a peaceful mass movement.

Should we repeat the programme and tactics of the non-co-operation movement? Not necessarily, but the basic idea must remain. Programmes and tactics must be made to fit in with circumstances, and it is neither easy nor desirable for this Congress at this stage to determine them in detail. That should be the work of its executive, the All-India Congress Committee. But the principles have to be fixed.

The old programme was one of the three boycotts—councils, law courts, and schools—leading up to refusal of service in the army and non-payment of taxes. When the national struggle is at its height I fail to see how it will be possible for any person engaged in it to continue in the courts or the schools. But still I think that it will be unwise to declare a boycott of the courts and schools at this stage.

The boycott of the legislative councils has led to much heated debate in the past, and this Congress itself has been rent in twain over it. We need not revive that controversy, for the circumstances to-day are entirely different. I feel that the step the Congress took some years ago to permit Congressmen to enter the councils was an inevitable step, and I am not prepared to say that some good has not resulted from it. But we have exhausted that good, and there is no middle course left to-day between boycott and full co-operation. All of us know the demoralization that these sham legislatures have brought in our ranks, and how many of our good men their committees and commissions lure away. Our workers are limited in number, and we can have no mass movement unless they concentrate on it and turn their backs on the palatial council-chambers of our legislatures. And if we declare for independence, how can we enter the councils and carry on our humdrum and profitless activities there? No programme or policy can be laid down for ever, nor can this Congress bind the country or even itself to pursue one line of action indefinitely. But to-day I would respectfully urge the Congress that the only policy in regard to the councils is a complete boycott of them. The All-India Congress Committee recommended this course in July last, and the time has come to give effect to it.

Our programme must, therefore, be one of political and economic boycott. It is not possible for us, so long as we are not actually independent, and not even then completely, to boycott another country wholly or to sever all connection with it. But our endeavour must be to reduce all points of contact with the British Government and to rely on ourselves. We must also make it clear that India will not accept responsibility for all the debts that England has piled on her. The Gaya Congress repudiated liability to pay these debts, and we must repeat this repudiation and stand by it.

Such of India's public debt as has been used for purposes beneficial to India we are prepared to admit and pay back. But we wholly deny all liability to pay back the vast sums which have been raised so that India may be held in subjection and her burdens may be increased. In particular, the poverty-stricken people of India cannot agree to shoulder the burden of the wars fought by England to extend her domain or consolidate her position in India. Nor can they accept the many concessions lavishly bestowed, without even proper compensation, on foreign exploiters.

This boycott will only be a means to an end. It will release energy and divert attention to the real struggle, which must take the shape of non-payment of taxes and, where possible, with the co-operation of the labour movement, general strikes. But non-payment of taxes must be well organized in specific areas, and for this purpose the Congress should authorize the All-India Congress Committee to take the necessary action wherever and whenever it considers desirable.

I have not, so far, referred to the constructive programme of the Congress. This should certainly continue, but the experience of the last few years shows us that by itself it does not carry us swiftly enough. It prepares the ground for future action, and ten years' silent work is bearing fruit to-day. In particular we shall, I hope, continue our boycott of foreign cloth and the boycott of British goods.

I have not referred so far to the Indians overseas and I do not propose to say much about them. This is not from any want of fellow-feeling with our brethren in East Africa or South Africa or Fiji or elsewhere, who are bravely struggling against great odds. But their fate will be decided in the plains of India, and the struggle we are launching into is as much for them as for ourselves.

For this struggle we want efficient machinery. Our Congress constitution and organization have become too archaic and slow moving, and are ill suited to times of crisis. The times of great demonstrations are past. We want quiet and irresistible action now, and this can only be brought about by the strictest discipline in our ranks. Our resolutions must be passed in order to be acted upon. The Congress will gain in strength, however small its actual membership may become, if it acts in a disciplined way. Small determined minorities have changed the fate of nations. Mobs and crowds can do little. Freedom itself involves restraint and discipline, and each one of us will have to subordinate himself to the larger good.

The Congress represents no small minority in the country, and though many may be too weak to join it or to work for it, they look to it with hope and longing to bring them deliverance. Ever since the Calcutta resolution the country has waited with anxious expectation for this great day when this Congress meets. None of us can say what and when we can achieve. We cannot command success. But success often comes to those who dare and act; it seldom goes to the timid who are ever afraid of the consequences. We play for high stakes; and if we seek to achieve great things it can only be through great dangers. Whether we succeed soon or late, none but ourselves can stop us from high endeavour and from writing a noble page in our country's long and splendid history.

We have conspiracy cases going on in various parts of the country. They are ever with us. But the time has gone for secret conspiracy. We have now an Open Conspiracy to free this country from foreign rule and you, comrades, and all our countrymen and countrywomen are invited to join it. But the rewards that are in store for you are suffering and prison and, it may be, death. But you shall also have the satisfaction that you have done your little bit for India, the ancient, but ever young, and have helped a little in the liberation of humanity from its present bondage.

Vande-Mataram! (Hail to the Motherland!)

2

WHITHER INDIA?*

NEVER in the long range of history has the world been in such a state of flux as it is to-day. Never has there been so much anxious questioning, so much doubt and bewilderment, so much examining of old institutions, existing ills, and suggested remedies. There is a continuous process of change and revolution going on all over the world, and everywhere anxious statesmen are almost at their wits' end and grope about in the dark. It is obvious that we are a part of this great world problem, and must be affected by world events. And yet, judging from the attention paid to these events in India, one would not think so. Major events are recorded in the news columns of papers, but little attempt is made to see behind and beneath them, to understand the forces that are shaking and reforming the world before our eyes, to comprehend the essential nature of social, economic, and political reality. History, whether past or present, becomes just a magic show with little rhyme or reason, and with no lesson for us which might guide our future path. On the gaily-decked official stage of India or England phantom figures come and go, posing for a while as great statesmen; Round Tablers flit about like pale shadows of those who created them, engaged in pitiful and interminable talk which interests few

* First published in India by Kitabistan, of Allahabad, in 1933.

and affects an even smaller number. Their main concern is how to save the vested interests of various classes or groups; their main diversion, apart from feasting, is self-praise. Others, blissfully ignorant of all that has happened in the last half-century, still talk the jargon of the Victorian Age and are surprised and resentful that nobody listens to them. Even the Nasmyth hammer of war and revolution and world change has failed to produce the slightest dent on their remarkably hard heads. Yet others hide vested interests under cover of communalism or even nationalism. And then there is the vague but passionate nationalism of many who find present conditions intolerable and hunger for national freedom without clearly realizing what form that freedom will take. And there are also here, as in many other countries, the usual accompaniments of a growing nationalism—an idealism, a mysticism, a feeling of exaltation, a belief in the mission of one's country, and something of the nature of religious revivalism. Essentially all these are middle-class phenomena.

Our politics must either be those of magic or of science. The former of course requires no argument or logic; the latter is in theory at least entirely based on clarity of thought and reasoning, and has no room for vague idealistic or religious or sentimental processes which confuse and befog the mind. Personally I have no faith in or use for the ways of magic and religion, and I can only consider the question on scientific grounds.

What, then, are we driving at? Freedom? Swaraj?

Independence? Dominion Status? Words which may mean much or little or nothing at all. Egypt is "independent," and yet, as everybody knows, it is at present little better than an Indian State, an autocracy imposed upon an unwilling people and propped up by the British. Economically, Egypt is a colony of some of the European imperialist Powers, notably the British. Ever since the World War there has been continuous conflict between Egyptian nationalism and the ruling authorities, and this continues to-day. So in spite of a so-called "independence" Egypt is very far from even national freedom.

Again, whose freedom are we particularly striving for, for nationalism covers many sins and includes many conflicting elements? There is the feudal India of the princes, the India of the big zamindars, of small zamindars, of the professional classes, of the agriculturists, of the industrialists, of the bankers, of the lower middle class, of the workers. There are the interests of foreign capital and those of home capital, of foreign services and home services. The nationalist answer is to prefer home interests to foreign interests, but beyond that it does not go. It tries to avoid disturbing the class divisions or the social *status quo*. It imagines that the various interests will somehow be accommodated when the country is free. Being essentially a middle-class movement, nationalism works chiefly in the interests of that class. It is obvious that there are serious conflicts between various interests in the country, and every law, every policy which is good for one interest may be harmful for another. What is good for the Indian prince may be thoroughly bad for the people of his State, what is profitable for the zamindar may ruin many of his tenants, what is demanded by foreign capital may crush the rising industries of the country.

Nothing is more absurd than to imagine that all the interests in the nation can be fitted in without injury to any. At every step some have to be sacrificed for others. A currency policy may be good for creditors or debtors, not for both at the same time. Inflation, resulting in a reduction or even wiping off of debts, will be welcomed by all debtors and by industry as a rule, but cursed by bankers and those who have fixed incomes. Early in the nineteenth century England deliberately sacrificed her agriculture for her rising industry. A few years ago, in 1925, by insisting on keeping the value of the pound sterling at par she sacrificed, to some extent, her industry to her banking and financial system, and faced industrial troubles and a huge general strike.

Any number of such instances can be given; they deal with the rival claims of different groups of the possessing classes. A more vital conflict of interests arises between these possessing classes as a whole and the others; between the Haves and Have-Nots. All this is obvious enough, but every effort is made to confuse the real issue by the holders of power, whether political or economic. The British Government is continually declaring before high heaven that they are trustees for our masses and India and England have common interests and can march hand in hand to a common destiny. Few people are taken in by this because nationalism makes us realize the inherent conflict between the two national interests. But nationalism does not make us realize the equally inherent and fundamental conflict between economic interests within the nation. There is an attempt to cover this up and avoid it on the ground that the national issue must be settled first. Appeals are issued for unity between different classes and groups to face the common national foe, and those who point out the inherent conflict between landlord and tenant, or capitalist and wage labourer, are criticized.

We may take it that the average person does not like conflict and continuous tension; he prefers peace and quiet, and is even prepared to sacrifice much for it. But the ostrich-like policy of refusing to see a conflict and a disorder which not only exist but are eating into society's vitals, to blind oneself to reality, will not end the conflict and the disorder, or suddenly change reality into unreality; for a politician or a man of action such a policy can only end in disaster. It is therefore essential that we keep this in mind and fashion our idea of freedom accordingly. We cannot escape having to answer the question, now or later, for the freedom of which class or classes in India are we especially striving? Do we place the masses, the peasantry and workers, first, or some other small class at the head of our list? Let us give the benefits of freedom to as many groups and classes as possible, but essentially whom do we stand for, and when a conflict arises whose side must we take? To say that we shall not answer that question now is itself an answer and taking of sides, for it means that we stand by the existing order, the *status quo*.

The form of government is after all a means to an end; even freedom itself is a means, the end being human well-being, human growth, the ending of poverty and disease and suffering, and the opportunity for every one to live the "good life," physically and mentally. What the "good life" is is a matter we cannot go into here, but most people will agree that freedom is essential to it—national freedom so far as the nation is concerned, personal freedom so far as the individual is concerned. For every restriction and inhibition stops growth and development, and produces, apart from economic disorders, complexes and perversions in the nation and individual. So freedom is necessary. Equally necessary is the will and the capacity for co-operation. Modern life grows so complex, there is so much interdependence, that co-operation is the very breath that keeps it functioning.

The long course of history shows us a succession of different forms of government and changing economic forms of production and organization. The two fit in and shape and influence each other. When economic change goes ahead too fast and the forms of government remain more or less static, a hiatus occurs, which is usually bridged over by a sudden change called revolution. The tremendous importance of economic events in shaping history and forms of government is now almost universally admitted.

We are often told that there is a world of difference

between the East and the West. The West is said to be materialistic, the East spiritual, religious, etc. What exactly the East signifies is seldom indicated, for the East includes the Bedouins of the Arabian deserts, the Hindus of India, the nomads of the Siberian Steppes, the pastoral tribes of Mongolia, the typically irreligious Confucians of China, and the Samurai of Japan. There are tremendous national and cultural differences between the different countries of Asia as well as of Europe; but there is no such thing as East and West except in the minds of those who wish to make this an excuse for imperialist domination, or those who have inherited such myths and fictions from a confused metaphysical past. Differences there are but they are chiefly due to different stages of economic growth.

We see, in north-western Europe, autocracy and feudalism giving place to the present capitalist order involving competition and large-scale production. The old small holdings disappear; the feudal checks on the serfs and cultivators go, and these agriculturists are also deprived of the little land they had. Large numbers of landless people are thrown out of employment and they have no land to fall back upon. A landless, propertyless proletariat is thus created. At the same time the checks and the controlled prices of the limited markets of feudal times disappear, and the open market appears. Ultimately this leads to the world market, the characteristic feature of capitalism.

Capitalism builds up on the basis of the landless proletariat, which could be employed as wage labourers in the factories, and the open market, where the machine-made goods could be sold. It grows rapidly and spreads all over the world. In the producing countries it was an active and living capitalism; in the colonial and consuming countries it was just a passive consumption of the goods made by machine industry in the West. North-western Europe, and a little later North America, exploit the resources of the world; they exploit Asia, Africa, East Europe, and South America. They add vastly to the wealth of the world, but this wealth is largely concentrated in a few nations and a few hands.

In this growth of capitalism, dominion over India was of vital importance to England. India's gold, in the early stages, helped in the further industrialization of England. And then India became a great producer of raw material to feed the factories of England and a huge market to consume the goods made in these factories. England, in her passionate desire to accumulate wealth, sacrificed her agriculture to her industry. England became almost a kind of vast city, and India the rural area attached to her.

The concentration of wealth in fewer hands went on. But the exploitation of India and other countries brought so much wealth to England that some of it trickled down to the working class and their standards of living rose. Working-class agitations were controlled and soothed by concessions from the capitalist owners, which they could well afford from the profits of imperialist exploitation. Wages rose; hours of work went down; there were insurance and other welfare schemes for the workers. A general prosperity in England took the edge off working-class discontent.

In India, passive industrialization meant an ever-growing burden on land. She became just a consumer of foreign machine-made goods. Her own cottage industries were partly destroyed forcibly, and partly by economic forces, and nothing took their place. All the ingredients and conditions for industrialization were present, but England did not encourage this, and indeed tried to prevent it by taxing machinery. And so the burden on the land grew and with it unemployment and poverty, and there was a progressive ruralization of India.

But the processes of history and economics cannot be stopped for long. Although general poverty was increasing, small groups accumulated some capital and wanted fields for investment. And so machine industry grew in India, partly with Indian capital, very much more so with foreign capital. Indian capital was largely dependent on foreign capital, and, in particular, could be controlled by the foreign banking system. It is well known that the World War gave a great push to Indian industry and afterwards, for reasons of imperial policy, England changed her policy towards Indian industry and began to encourage it, but mostly with foreign capital. The growth of so-called swadeshi industries in India thus represented to a very great extent the increasing hold of British capital on India.

The growth of industries and nationalist movements in all the countries of the East checked Western exploitation, and the profits of Western capitalism began to go down. War debts and other consequences of the war were a tremendous burden for all the countries concerned. There was not so much money or profits of industry to be distributed to the working class in the West, and the discontent and pressure of the workers grew. There was also the living incentive and inspiration of the Russian Revolution for the workers.

Meanwhile two other processes were working silently but with great rapidity. One was the concentration of wealth and industrial power in fewer hands by the formation of huge trusts, cartels, and combines. The other was a continuous improvement in technique in the methods of production, leading to greater mechanization, far greater production, and more unemployment as workers were replaced by machinery. And this led to a curious result. Just when industry was producing goods on the biggest mass scale in history, there were few people to buy them, as the great majority were too poor to be able to afford them. The armies of the unemployed were not earning anything, so how could they spend? and even the majority of those earning had little to spare. A new truth suddenly dawned on the perplexed minds of the great captains of industry (this dawning process has not yet taken place among the leaders of industry in India), and the truth was this: that mass production necessitates mass consumption. But if the masses have no money how are they to buy or consume? And what of production then? So production is stopped or restricted and the wheels of industry slow down till they barely move. Unemployment grows all the more, and this again makes consumption diminish.

This is the crisis of capitalism which has had the world by the throat for over four years. Essentially it is due to the ill distribution of the world's wealth; to its concentration in a few hands. And the disease seems to be of the essence of capitalism and grows with it till it eats and destroys the very system which created it. There is no lack of money in the world, no lack of foodstuffs, or the many other things that man requires. The world is richer to-day than it has ever been, and holds promise of untold advance in the near future. And yet the system breaks down, and while millions starve and endure privation huge quantities of foodstuffs and other articles are destroyed, insect pests are let loose on the fields to destroy crops, harvests are not gathered, and nations meet together to confer how to restrict future crops of wheat and cotton and tea and coffee and many other articles. From the beginning of history man has fought with nature to get the barest necessities of life, and now that nature's wealth is poured out before him, enough to remove poverty for ever from the world, his only way of dealing with it is to burn and destroy it, and become poorer and more destitute in the process.

History has never offered a more amazing paradox. It seems clear enough that the capitalist system of industry, whatever its services in the past may have been, is no longer suited to the present methods of production. Technical advance has gone far ahead of the existing social structure, and, as in the past, this hiatus causes most of our present-day disorders. Till that lag is made up and a new system in keeping with the new technique is adopted, the disorders are likely to continue. The change over to the new system is of course opposed by those who have vested interests in the old system, and though this old system is dying before their eyes they prefer to hold on to their little rather than share a lot with others.

It is not, fundamentally, a moral issue, as some people imagine, although there is a moral side to it. It is not a question of blaming capitalism or cursing capitalists and the like. Capitalism has been of the greatest service to the world, and individual capitalists are but tiny wheels in the big machine. The question now is whether the capitalist system has not outlived its day and must now give place to a better and a saner ordering of human affairs, which is more in keeping with the progress of science and human knowledge.

In India, during this period, the tremendous burden on land continued and even increased, despite the growth of industry in certain areas. Economic discontent increased. The middle class grew up and, finding no sufficient scope for self-development, demanded political changes and took to agitation. More or less similar causes worked all over the colonial and dependent East. Especially after the war, national movements grew rapidly in Egypt and most of the countries of Asia. These movements were essentially due to the distress of the masses and the lower middle classes. There was a strange similarity even in the methods employed by these movements—non-co-operation, boycotts of legislatures, boycotts of goods, *hartals*, strikes, etc. Occasionally there were violent outbreaks, as in Egypt and Syria, but stress was laid far more on peaceful methods. In India, of course, non-violence was made a basic principle by the Congress at the suggestion of Gandhiji.* All these national struggles for freedom have continued till now, and they are bound to continue till a solution of the basic problem is found. Fundamentally, this solution is not merely a question of satisfying the natural desire for self-rule, but one of filling hungry stomachs.

The great revolutionary nationalist urge in Asia of the after-war years gradually exhausted itself for the time being and conditions stabilized themselves. In India this took the form of the Swarajist entry into the Assembly and the Councils. In Europe also the middle nineteen-twenties was a period of settling down and adaptation to the new conditions created by the World War. The revolution that had hovered all over Europe in 1919 and 1920 failed to come off and receded into the background. American gold poured into Europe and revived to some extent the war-weary and disillusioned peoples of that continent, and created a false appearance of prosperity. But this prosperity had no real basis and the crash came in 1929, when the United States of America stopped lending money to Europe and South America. Many

* Here, as in some other places, Mr. Nehru gives Mr. Gandhi the familiar Indian title "Gandhiji. The "ji" denotes respect, and is almost comparable to "Mr."

factors, and especially the inherent conflicts of a declining capitalism, contributed to this crash, and the house of cards of after-war capitalist prosperity began to tumble down. That process of tumbling down has been going on at a tremendous pace for four years, and there is no end to it yet. It is called the slump, trade depression, the crisis, etc., but it is really the evening of the capitalist system, and the world is being compelled by circumstances to recognize this. International trade is reaching vanishing point, international co-operation has failed, the world-market which was the essential basis of capitalism is disappearing, and each nation is trying frantically to shift for itself at the cost of others. Whatever the future may bring, one thing is certain: that the old order has gone and all the king's horses and all the king's men will not set it up again.

As the old capitalist order has tottered the challenge to it by the growing forces of labour has grown more intense. This challenge, when it has become dangerous, has induced the possessing classes to sink their petty differences and band themselves together to fight the common foe. This has led to Fascism and, in its milder forms, to the formation of so-called national governments. Essentially, these are the last ditch efforts of the possessing classes, or the "kept classes"[1] as they have been called by an American economist, to hold on to what they have. The struggle becomes more intense and the forms of nineteenth-century democracy are discarded. But Fascism or national governments offer no solution of the fundamental economic inconsistencies of the present-day capitalist system, and so long as they do not remove the inequalities of wealth and solve the problem of distribution they are doomed to fail. Of the major capitalist countries the United States of America is the only place where some attempt is being made to-day towards lessening to a slight extent inequalities in wealth by State action. Carried to a logical conclusion, President Roosevelt's programme will lead to a form of State Socialism; it is far more likely that the effort will fail and result in Fascism. England, as is her habit, is grimly muddling through and waiting for something to happen. Meanwhile she has derived considerable help from India's gold and resources. But all this is temporary relief only and the nations slide downhill and approach the brink.

Thus, if we survey the world to-day, we find that capitalism, having solved the problem of production, helplessly faces the allied problem of distribution and is unable to solve it. It was not in the nature of the capitalist system to deal satisfactorily with distribution, and production alone makes the world top-heavy and unbalanced. To find a solution for distributing wealth and purchasing power evenly is to put an end to the basic inequalities of the capitalist system and to replace capitalism itself by a more scientific system.

Capitalism has led to imperialism and to the conflicts of imperialist powers in search for colonial areas for exploitation, for areas of raw produce and for markets for manufactured goods. It has led to ever-increasing conflicts with the rising nationalism of colonial countries, and to social conflicts with powerful movements of the exploited working class. It has resulted in recurrent crises, political and economic, leading to economic and tariff wars as well as political wars on an enormous scale. Every subsequent crisis is on a bigger scale than the previous one, and now we live in a perpetual state of crisis and slump and the shadow of war darkens the horizon.

And yet it is well to remember that the world to-day has a surfeit of food and the other good things of life. Terrible want exists because the present system does not know how to distribute them. Repeated international conferences have failed to find a way out because they represented the claims of vested interests and dared not touch the system itself. They grope blindly in the dark in their stuffy rooms while the foundations of the house they built are being sapped by the advance of science and economic events. Everywhere thinkers have recognized the utter inadequacy of the existing system, though they have differed as to the remedies. Communists and Socialists point with confidence to the way of Socialism and they are an ever-growing power for they have science and logic on their side. In America a great stir was caused recently by the Technocrats, a group of engineers who want to do away with money itself and to substitute for it a unit of energy, an erg. In England the social credit theories of Major Douglas, according to which the whole production of the nation will be evenly distributed to the whole population—a kind of "dividends for all"—find increasing acceptance. Barter takes the place of trade both in the domestic and the international market. The growth of these revolutionary theories even among the well-to-do classes, and especially the intellectuals, is in itself an indication of the tremendous change in mentality that is taking place in the world. How many of us can conceive a world without money and with the invisible erg as its measure of value? And yet this is soberly and earnestly advocated not by wild agitators but by well-known economists and engineers.

This is the world background.

The Asiatic background is intimately related to this and yet it has its peculiar features. Asia is the main field of conflict between nationalism and imperialism. Asia is still undeveloped as compared to Europe and North America. It has a vast population which can consume goods if they had the necessary purchasing power to do so. To the hard-pressed imperialist Powers seeking frantically for areas of economic expansion, Asia still offers a field, though nationalism offers many obstructions. Hence the talk of a "push to Asia" to find an outlet for the surplus goods of the West and thus stabilize Western capitalism for another period. Capitalism is a young and growing force in the East; it has not, as in India, wholly overthrown feudalism yet. But even before capitalism had established itself other forces, inimical to it, have risen to challenge it. And it is obvious that if capitalism collapses in Europe and America it cannot survive in Asia.

Nationalism is still the strongest force in Asia (we

can ignore for our present purpose the Soviet territories of Asia). This is natural as a country under alien domination must inevitably think first in terms of nationalism. But the powerful economic forces working for change in the world to-day have influenced this nationalism to an ever-increasing extent, and everywhere it is appearing in Socialistic garb. Gradually the nationalist struggle for political freedom is becoming a social struggle also for economic freedom. Independence and the Socialist State become the objectives, with varying degrees of stress being laid on the two aspects of the problem. As political freedom is delayed, the other aspect assumes greater importance, and it now seems probable, especially because of world conditions, that political and social emancipation will come together to some at least of the countries of Asia.

That is the Asiatic background.

In India, as in other Asiatic colonial countries, we find a struggle to-day between the old nationalist ideology and the new economic ideology. Most of us have grown up under the nationalist tradition, and it is hard to give up the mental habits of a lifetime. And yet we realize that this outlook is inadequate; it does not fit in with existing conditions in our country or in the world; there is a hiatus, a lag. We try to bridge this hiatus, but the process of crossing over to a new ideology is always a painful one. Many of us are confused and perplexed to-day because of this. But the crossing has to be made, unless we are to remain in a stagnant backwater, overwhelmed from time to time by the wash of the boats that move down the river of progress. We must realize that the nineteenth century cannot solve the problems of the twentieth, much less can the seventh century or earlier ages do so.

Having glanced at the general background of Asia and the world we can have a clearer view of our own national problem. India's freedom affects each one of us intimately, and we are apt to look upon it as a thing apart and unconnected with world events. But the Indian problem is a part of the Asiatic problem and is tied up with the problems of the world. We cannot, even if we will it, separate it from the rest. What happens in India will affect the world and world events will change India's future. Indeed it may be said that the three great world problems to-day are: the fate of capitalism, which means the fate of Europe and America, the future of India, and the future of China, and all these are interrelated.

India's struggle to-day is part of the great struggle which is going on all over the world for the emancipation of the oppressed. Essentially, this is an economic struggle, with hunger and want as its driving forces, although it puts on nationalist and other dresses.

Indian freedom is necessary because the burden on the Indian masses as well as the middle classes is too heavy to be borne, and must be lightened or done away with. The measure of freedom is the extent to which this burden is removed. This burden is due to the vested interests of a foreign government as well as those of certain groups and classes in India and abroad. The achievement of freedom thus becomes a question, as Gandhiji said recently, of divesting vested interests. If an indigenous government took the place of the foreign government and kept all the vested interests intact, this would not even be the shadow of freedom.

We have got into an extraordinary habit of thinking of freedom in terms of paper constitutions. Nothing could be more absurd than this lawyer's mentality which ignores life and the vital economic issues and can only proceed on the basis of the *status quo* and precedents. Too much reliance on past practice has somehow succeeded in twisting the lawyer's head backwards and he seems to be incapable of looking ahead. Even the halt and the lame go slowly forward; not so the lawyer who is convinced, like the fanatic in religion, that truth can only lie in the past.

The Round Table scheme is almost as dead as Queen Anne and hardly deserves notice. It was not meant to give an iota of freedom to the Indian people; it sought to win over certain Indian vested interests to the British side and in this it succeeded. It answered, to the satisfaction of its votaries, the question I had formulated at the beginning of this essay: whose freedom are we striving for? It gave greater protection and assurance and freedom to the British vested interests in India. It was Home Rule for the Viceroy, as Mr. Vithalbhai Patel said. It confirmed the interests of British capital and British services and, in some cases, gave them even more than they have now. It tried to perpetuate the alien military occupation of India. Further, it gave greater freedom and importance to the vested interests of the princes and the semi-feudal magnates. In brief, the whole scheme was meant for the protection and perpetuation of the numerous vested interests that exploit the Indian masses. Having done this useful and, to themselves, profitable piece of work, the originators of the scheme told us that autonomy was a costly affair and would mean the expenditure of many extra millions for each province! Thus not only were all the old burdens on the masses to be continued, but many new ones were to be added. This was the ingenious solution discovered by the wise and learned men who foregathered at the Round Table Conference. Intent on protecting their class privileges they happened to forget an odd three hundred and fifty million people in India.

Even a child in politics can point out the folly of this procedure. The whole basis and urge of the national movement came from a desire for economic betterment, to throw off the burdens that crushed the masses, and to end the exploitation of the Indian people. If these burdens continue and are actually added to, it does not require a powerful mind to realize that the fight must not only continue but grow more intense. Leaders and individuals may come and go; they may get tired and slacken off; they may compromise or betray; but the exploited and suffering masses must carry on the struggle, for their drill-sergeant is hunger. Swaraj or freedom from exploitation for them is not a fine paper constitution or a problem of the hereafter. It is a question of the here and now, of immediate relief. Roast lamb and mint sauce may be a tasty dish for those who eat it, but the poor lamb is not likely to appreciate the force of the best of arguments which point out the beauty of sacrifice for the good of the elect and the joys of close communion, even though dead, with mint sauce.

India's immediate goal can therefore only be considered in terms of the ending of the exploitation of her people. Politically, it must mean independence and the severance of the British connection, which means imperialist dominion; economically and socially it must mean the ending of all special class privileges and vested interests. The whole world is struggling to this end; India can do no less, and in this way the Indian struggle for freedom lines up with the world struggle. Is our aim human welfare or the preservation of class privileges and the vested interests of pampered groups? The question must be answered clearly and unequivocally by each one of us. There is no room for quibbling when the fate of nations and millions of human beings is at stake. The day for palace intrigues and parlour politics and pacts and compromises passes when the masses enter politics. Their manners are not those of the drawing-room; we never took the trouble to teach them any manners. Their school is the school of events and suffering is their teacher. They learn their politics from great movements which bring out the true nature of individuals and classes, and the civil disobedience movement has taught the Indian masses many a lesson which they will never forget.

Independence is a much-abused word and it hardly connotes what we are driving at. And yet there is no other suitable word and, for want of a better, we must use it. National isolation is neither a desirable nor a possible ideal in a world which is daily becoming more of a unit. International and intranational activities dominate the world and nations are growing more and more interdependent. Our ideal and objective cannot go against this historical tendency, and we must be prepared to discard a narrow nationalism in favour of world co-operation and real internationalism. Independence therefore cannot mean for us isolation but freedom from all imperialist control, and because Britain to-day represents imperialism, our freedom can only come after the British connection is severed. We have no quarrel with the British people, but between British imperialism and Indian freedom there is no meeting ground and there can be no peace. If imperialism goes from Britain we shall gladly co-operate with her in the wider international field; not otherwise.

British statesmen of the Liberal and Labour variety often point out to us the ills of a narrow nationalism and dwell on the virtues of what used to be known as the British Empire and is now euphemistically called the British Commonwealth of Nations. Under cover of fine and radical words and phrases they seek to hide the ugly and brutal face of imperialism and try to keep us in its embrace of death. Some Indian public men, who ought to know better, also praise the virtues of internationalism, meaning thereby the British Empire, and tell us in sorrow how narrow-minded we are in demanding independence, in place of that wonderful thing (which nobody offers us)

Dominion Status. The British, it is well known, have a remarkable capacity for combining their moral instincts with their self-interest. That is perhaps not unnatural, but it is remarkable how some of our own countrymen are taken in by this unctuous and hypocritical attitude. Even the light of day is wasted on those who keep their eyes shut. It is worth noting, however, that the foreign policy of England has been the greatest stumbling-block to international co-operation through the League of Nations or otherwise. All the European and American world knows this, but most of us, who look at foreign politics through English spectacles, have not grasped this fact yet. Disarmament, air-bombing, the attitude to the Manchurian question, are some of the recent witnesses to England's attitude. Even the Kellogg-Briand Pact of Paris, which was to have outlawed war, was only accepted by England subject to certain qualifications and reservations regarding her empire, which effectively nullified the Pact. The British Empire and real internationalism are as the poles apart, and it is not through that empire that we can march to internationalism.

The real question before us, and before the whole world, is one of fundamental change of regime politically, economically, socially. Only thus can we put India on the road to progress and stop the progressive deterioration of our country. In a revolutionary period, such as exists in the world to-day, it is foolish waste of energy to think and act in terms of carrying on the existing regime and trying to reform it and improve it. To do so is to waste the opportunity which history offers once in a long while. "The whole world is in revolution," says Mussolini. "Events themselves are a tremendous force pushing us on like some implacable will." Individuals, however eminent, play but a minor role when the world is on the move. They may divert the main current here and there to some slight extent; they may not and cannot stop the rushing torrent. And therefore the only peace that can endure is with circumstances, not merely with men.

Whither India? Surely to the great human goal of social and economic equality, to the ending of all exploitation of nation by nation and class by class, to national freedom within the framework of an international co-operative Socialist world federation. This is not such an empty idealist dream as some people imagine. It is within the range of the practical politics of to-day and the near future. We may not have it within our grasp, but those with vision can see it emerging on the horizon. And even if there be delay in the realization of our goal, what does it matter if our steps march in the right direction and our eyes look steadily in front? For in the pursuit itself of a mighty purpose there is joy and happiness and a measure of achievement. As Bernard Shaw has said: "This is the true joy in life, the being used for a purpose recognized by yourself as a mighty one; the being thoroughly worn out before you are thrown on the scrapheap; the being a force of nature, instead of a feverish, selfish little clod of ailments and grievances, complaining that the world will not devote itself to making you happy."

3

PRESIDENTIAL ADDRESS TO THE NATIONAL CONGRESS, LUCKNOW, APRIL, 1936

AFTER many years I face you again from this tribune—many weary years of strife and turmoil and common suffering. It is good for us to meet again; it is good for me to see this great host of old comrades and friends, linked together by strong bonds that cannot break, to sense the old brave spirit yet again, to feel your overwhelming kindness and goodwill to one whose greatest privilege it is to have been a comrade and a soldier with all of you in a mighty struggle for freedom. I am heartened and strengthened by you, though even in this great gathering I feel a little lonely. Many a dear comrade and friend has left us, worn out, long before the normal length of our earthly days, by the stress and strain of conflict. One by one they go, leaving a void in our hearts and a dull misery in our minds. They find peace from this turmoil perhaps, and it is well, for they deserved it. They rest after their labours.

But what of us who remain behind with a heavier burden to carry? There is no rest for us or for those who languish in prison or in detention camp. We cannot rest, for rest is betrayal of those who have gone and in going handed the torch of freedom to us to keep alight; it is betrayal of the cause we have espoused and the pledge we have taken; it is betrayal of the millions who never rest.

I am aweary and I have come back like a tired child yearning for solace in the bosom of our common mother, India. That solace has come to me in overflowing measure; thousands of hands have been stretched out to me in love and sympathy; millions of silent voices have carried their message of affection to my heart. How can I thank you, men and women of India? How can I express in words feelings that are too deep for utterance?

For many years now I have been a distant looker-on on this Indian scene where once I was an actor, and many a thing has happened that has filled me with distress and anguish. I do not wish to survey this recent past of ours, which must be fresh in your memory, and which has left a sorry trail behind and many knots which are difficult to unravel. But we may not ignore it for out of that past as well as the present, we have to build our future. We have followed high ideals and we have taken pride in the fact that our means are worthy of those ideals. We have been witnesses of many a miracle in this old and battered land of ours, and yet our very success has been followed by failure and disillusion. Temporary failure has little significance when the aim is high and the struggle bound to be a long one; it is but the incentive to further effort. Often it teaches us more than a victory easily won and becomes a prelude to a greater success. But we profit by it only if we learn its lesson and search our minds for an explanation of that failure. Only by constant self-questioning, individual and national, can we keep on the right path. An easy and unthinking confidence is almost as bad as a weak submission to helpless dejection. Real failure comes only when we forget our ideals and objectives and principles and begin to wander away from the road which leads to their realization.

In this crisis of our history, therefore, let us look into ourselves and examine, without pity or prejudice, what we have done and what others have done to us, and seek to find out where we stand to-day. We dare not delude ourselves or evade real issues for fear of offending others, even though some of these others are comrades whom we respect. That is the way of self-deception which none who seek great and vital changes can follow except at their peril.

Sixteen years ago, under the inspiration of our leader, we took a new and long step converting this Congress from an ineffective body, feebly functioning amongst the upper classes, into a powerful democratic organization with its roots in the Indian soil and the vast masses who live on it. A handful of our old friends, representing an age and a class which had had its day, left us, fearful of this democratic upsurge, and preferring the shelter and protection of British imperialism to joining hands with the new vital forces which convulsed the country and struggled for freedom. Historically, they lapsed into the past. But we heard the rumbling of those forces and, for the moment, lined up with them and played a not unworthy part in current history. We sensed the new spirit of mass release, of psychological escape from the cramping effects of long subjection; we gloried in the breaking of the mental bonds that encompassed us. And because our minds became free we felt that political freedom could not be far, for it is often harder to break the bonds of the spirit than physical bonds and chains of iron and steel. We represented the Spirit of the Age and were marching step by step with countless others in our country and outside. The exhilaration of being in tune with the masses and with world forces came upon us, and the feeling that we were the agents of historic destiny.

We were engrossed in our national struggle, and the turn it took bore the powerful impress of our great leader and of our national genius. We were hardly conscious then of what was happening outside. And yet our struggle was but part of a far wider struggle for freedom, and the forces that moved us were moving millions of people all over the world and driving them into action. All Asia was astir from the Mediterranean to the Far East, from the Islamic West to the Buddhist East; Africa responded to the new spirit; Europe, broken up by the war, was struggling to find a new equilibrium. And right across a vast area in Europe and Asia,* in the Soviet territories, a new conception of human freedom and social equality fought desperately against a host of enemies. There were great differences in the many aspects of this freedom struggle all over the world, and we were misled by them and did not see the common background. Yet if we are to understand these varied phenomena, and derive a lesson from them for our own national struggle, we must try to see and understand the whole picture. And if we do so we cannot fail to observe an organic connection between them which endures through changing situations. If once we grasp this organic bond, the world situation becomes easier to understand and our own national problems take their proper places in the wider picture. We realize then that we cannot isolate India or the Indian problem from that of the rest of the world. To do so is to ignore the real forces that are shaping events and to cut ourselves adrift from the vital energy that flows from them. To do so, again, is to fail to understand the significance of our own problems, and if we do not understand this how can we solve them? We are apt to lose ourselves, as we have indeed done, in petty conflicts and minor questions, like the communal problem, and forget the major issues; we are apt to waste our energy (like our moderate friends do) in interminable discussions over legal quibbles and constitutional questions.

During the troubled aftermath of the Great War came revolutionary changes in Europe and Asia, and the intensification of the struggle for social freedom in Europe, and a new aggressive nationalism in the countries of Asia. There were ups and downs, and sometimes it appeared as if the revolutionary urge had exhausted itself and things were settling down. But economic and political conditions were such that there could be no settling down, the existing structure could no longer cope with these new conditions, and all its efforts to do so were vain and fruitless. Everywhere conflicts grew, and a great depression overwhelmed the world and there was a progressive deterioration, everywhere except in the wide-flung Soviet territories of the U.S.S.R., where, in marked contrast with the rest of the world, astonishing progress was made in every direction. Two rival economic and political systems faced each other in the world and, though they tolerated each other for a while, there was an inherent antagonism between them, and they played for mastery on the stage of the world. One of them was the capitalist order which had inevitably developed into vast imperialisms, which, having swallowed the colonial world, were intent on eating each other up. Powerful still and fearful of war, which might endanger their possessions, yet they came into inevitable conflict with each other and prepared feverishly for war. They were quite unable to solve the problems that threatened them, and helplessly they submitted to slow decay. The other was the Socialist order of the U.S.S.R. which went from progress to progress, though often at terrible cost, and where the problems of the capitalist world had ceased to exist.

Capitalism, in its difficulties, took to Fascism with all its brutal suppression of what Western civilization had apparently stood for; it became, even in some of its homelands, what its imperialist counterpart had long been in the subject colonial countries. Fascism and imperialism thus stood out as the two faces of the new decaying capitalism, and though they varied in different countries according to national characteristics and economic and political conditions, they represented the same forces of reaction and supported each other, and at the same time came into conflict with each other, for such conflict was inherent in their very nature. Socialism in the West, and the rising nationalisms of the Eastern and other dependent countries, opposed this combination of Fascism and imperialism. Nationalism in the East, it must be remembered, was essentially different from the new and terribly narrow nationalism of Fascist countries; the former was the historical urge to freedom, the latter the last refuge of reaction.

Thus we see the world divided up into two vast groups to-day—the imperialist and Fascist on one side, the Socialist and nationalist on the other. There is some overlapping of the two and the line between them is difficult to draw, for there is mutual conflict between the Fascist and imperialist Powers, and the nationalism of subject countries has sometimes a tendency to Fascism. But the main division holds, and if we keep it in mind, it will be easier for us to understand world conditions and our own place in them.

Where do we stand, then, we who labour for a free India? Inevitably we take our stand with the progressive forces of the world which are ranged against Fascism and imperialism. We have to deal with one imperialism in particular, the oldest and the most far-reaching of the modern world, but powerful as it is, it is but one aspect of world-imperialism. And that is the final argument for Indian independence and for the severance of our connection with the British Empire.

Between Indian nationalism, Indian freedom, and British imperialism there can be no common ground, and if we remain within the imperialist fold, whatever our name or status, whatever outward semblance of political power we might have, we remain cribbed and confined and allied to and dominated by the reactionary forces and the great financial vested interests of the capitalist world. The exploitation of our masses will still continue and all the vital social problems that face us will remain unsolved. Even real political freedom will be out of our reach, much more so radical social changes.

With the development of this great struggle all over the world we have seen the progressive deterioration of many of the capitalist-imperialist countries, and an attempt at consolidation of the reactionary forces under Fascism or Naziism or so-called "national" governments. In India the same process has been evident to us during these past years, and the stronger the nationalist movement has grown, the more have efforts been made by our imperialist rulers to break our ranks and to gather together under their banner the reactionary elements in the country. The Round Table Conferences were such attempts and, though they helped our rulers in some measure, they served a useful purpose by showing us clearly the division between the imperialist and the anti-imperialist forces in the country. Unhappily we did not fully profit by this lesson, and we still imagine that we can win over some of these imperialist groups to the side of Indian freedom and anti-imperialism, and in a vain attempt to do so, we suppress our ideals, blush for our objectives, and tone down our activities.

Meanwhile the decay of British imperialism in India becomes ever more apparent. It cannot, by its very nature, solve our economic problems and rid us of our terrible poverty, which it has largely itself created. It subsists on a normal fare of the fiercest repression and a denial of civil and even personal liberty. It surrounds us with a wide network of spies and, among the pillars of its administration, are the tribe of informers and *agents provocateurs* and the like. Its services try to seek comfort for their obvious deterioration and incompetence by perpetually singing songs of mutual adulation. Argument gives place to the policeman's baton and the soldier's bayonet and prison and detention camp, and even our extraordinary finances are justified by the methods of the bully. It is astonishing to find to what depths of vulgarity our rulers have descended in their ardent desire to hold on to what they have got, and it is depressing, though perhaps inevitable, that some of our own countrymen, more interested in British imperialism than the British themselves, should excel at this deplorable game. So wanting in mental equilibrium are they, so obsessed by fear of the Congress and the national movement it represents, that their wishes become thoughts, their thoughts inferences, and their inferences facts, solemnly stated in official publications, and on which the majesty of the British Government rests in India, and people are kept in prison and detention camps without charge or trial. Being interested in psychology, I have watched this process of moral and intellectual decay and realized, even more than I did previously, how autocratic power corrupts and degrades and vulgarizes. I have read sometimes the reports of the recent Assembly meetings and noted the great difference in tone and content between them and the Assembly of ten years ago. I have observed the forced attempts made to discredit the Congress by a reference to the Tilak Swaraj Fund with which I was connected for many years as Secretary of the Congress. But prepared as I was for much, even I was surprised at the insinuations made against our much-loved chief, Rajendra Babu, and the charges brought against the Behar Relief Fund. A mild criticism by me of official incompetence soon after the Behar earthquake was deeply resented probably because the truth of it was realized. Newspapers that criticized the official arrangements at a subsequent earthquake were heavily penalized or suppressed. All criticism hurts the sensitive skin of the Government, and its reactions are quick and far-reaching. The more incompetent it grows the less it likes being told so. But this does not prevent it from indulging in reckless allegations about others.

This psychological aspect interests me even more than the more aggressive manifestations of British authority in India, for it throws light on much that has happened. It shows us how a clear and definite Fascist mentality has developed among our rulers and how closely allied is imperialism to Fascism. How this Fascist mentality has functioned in the recent past and is functioning to-day I shall not go into now. You know well the horror of these years and of the nightmare that we have all experienced. We shall not easily forget it, and if there are some who have been cowed down by it, there are others who have steeled themselves to a greater resolve to end this infamy in India.

But of one thing I must say a few words, for to me it is one of the most vital things that I value. That is the tremendous deprivation of civil liberties in India. A Government that has to rely on the Criminal Law Amendment Act and similar laws, that suppresses the press and literature, that bans hundreds of organizations, that keeps people in prison without trial, and that does so many other things that are happening in India to-day, is a Government that has ceased to have even a shadow of a justification for its existence. I can never adjust myself to these conditions, I find them intolerable. And yet I find many of my own countrymen complacent about them, some even supporting them, some, who have made the practice of sitting on a fence into a fine art, being neutral when such questions are discussed. And I have wondered what there was in common between them and me and those who think as I do. We in the Congress welcome all co-operation in the struggle for Indian freedom; our doors are ever open to all who stand for that freedom and are against imperialism. But they are not open to the allies of imperialism and the supporters of repression and those who stand by the British Government in its suppression of civil liberty. We belong to opposite camps.

Recently, as you know, we have had a typical

example of the way Government functions in India in the warning issued to a dear and valued comrade of ours, Subhas Chandra Bose. We who know him also know how frivolous are the charges brought against him. But even if there was substance in them we could not tolerate willingly the treatment to which he has long been subjected. He did me the honour to ask me for advice and I was puzzled and perplexed, for it is no easy thing to advise another in such a matter, when such advice might mean prison. Subhas Bose has suffered enough at the cost of his health. Was I justified in adding to this mental and physical agony? I hesitated and at first suggested to him to postpone his departure. But this advice made me unhappy, and I consulted other friends and then advised him differently. I suggested that he should return to his homeland as soon as he could. But, it appears, that even before my advice reached him, he had started on his journey back to India.

This instance leads us to think of the larger problem, of the way the bogey of terrorism has been exploited by the Government to crush political activity and to cripple physically and mentally the fair province of Bengal. You know that terrorism as such is practically non-existent now in Bengal or any part of India. Terrorism is always a sign of political immaturity in a people, just as so-called constitutionalism, where there is no democratic constitution, is a sign of political senility. Our national movement has long outgrown that immature stage, and even the odd individuals who have in the past indulged in terrorist acts have apparently given up that tragic and futile philosophy. The Congress, by its stress on peaceful and effective action, has drawn the youth of the country into its fold, and all traces of terroristic activity would long have vanished but for the policy of the Government which feeds the roots out of which a helpless violence grows. But terrorism or no terrorism, a Government which adopts the methods which have long prevailed in Midnapore and elsewhere in Bengal stands self-condemned. Similar methods have also long prevailed in the Frontier Province, although there is no hint of terroristic activity there, and that fine man and true, beloved of millions, Abdul Ghaffar Khan, still lies in prison. Excuses differ, but the real reason is the ever-growing Fascist mentality of our rulers.

That is one side of the picture. What of us? I have found a spirit of disunion spreading over the land, a strange *malaise*, and petty conflicts amongst old comrades growing ever bigger and interfering with all activity. We have forgotten for the moment the larger ideals we stood for, and we quarrel over petty issues. We have largely lost touch with the masses and, deprived of the life-giving energy that flows from them, we dry up and weaken and our organization shrinks and loses the power it had. First things must always come first, and because we have forgotten this and argue and dispute over secondary matters, we are in danger of losing our bearings.

Every great struggle has its ups and downs and temporary failures. When such a setback occurs there is a reaction when the fund of national energy is exhausted and has to be re-charged. That happens again and again, and yet that is not an adequate explanation of all that has taken place. Our direct-action struggles in the past were based on the masses, and especially the peasantry, but the backbone and leadership were always supplied by the middle classes, and this, under the circumstances, was inevitable. The middle classes are a vague group or groups; at the top, a handful of them are closely allied to British imperialism; at the bottom are the dispossessed and other groups who have been progressively crushed by economic circumstances and out of whose ranks come the advanced political workers and revolutionaries; in between are the centre groups, which tend often to side with the advanced elements, but which also have alliances with the upper groups and live in the hope of joining their superior ranks. A middle-class leadership is thus often a distracted leadership, looking in two directions at the same time. In times of crisis and struggle, when unity of aim and activity is essential, this two-faced leadership is bound to injure the cause and to hold back when a forward move is called for. Being too much tied up with property and the goods of this world, it is fearful of losing them, and it is easier to bring pressure on it and to exhaust its stamina. And yet, paradoxically, it is only from the middle class intellectuals that revolutionary leadership comes, and we in India know that our bravest leaders and our stoutest comrades have come from the ranks of the middle classes. But by the very nature of our struggle, these front-rank leaders are taken away and the others who take their place tire and are influenced more by the static element of their class. That has been very evident during our recent struggle when our propertied classes were hit hard by the Government's drastic policy of seizure and confiscation of monies and properties, and were thus induced to bring pressure for the suspension of the struggle.

How is this problem to be solved, then? Inevitably, we must have middle-class leadership, but this must look more and more towards the masses and draw strength and inspiration from them. The Congress must be not only *for* the masses, as it claims to be, but *of* the masses; only then will it really be for the masses. I have a feeling that our relative weakness to-day is due to a certain decay of our middle-class elements and our divorce from the people at large. Our policies and ideas are governed far more by this middle-class outlook than by a consideration of the needs of the great majority of the population. Even the problems that trouble us are essentially middle-class problems, like the communal problem, which have no significance for the masses.

This is partly due, I think, to a certain historical growth during the last fifteen years to which we have failed to adapt ourselves, to a growing urgency of economic problems affecting the masses, and to a rising mass consciousness which does not find sufficient outlet through the Congress. This was not so in 1920 and later, when there was an organic link between Congress and the masses, and their needs and desires, vague as they were, found expression in the Congress. But as those needs and desires have taken more definite shape, they have not been so welcome to other elements in the Congress and that organic connection has gone. That, though regrettable, is really a sign of growth and, instead of lamenting it, we must find a new link and a new connection on a fresh basis which allows for growth of mass consciousness within the Congress. The middle-class claim to represent the masses had some justification in 1920; it has much less to-day, though the lower middle classes have still a great deal in common with the masses.

Partly also our divorce from the people at large is due to a certain narrowness of our Congress constitution. The radical changes made in it fifteen years ago brought it in line with existing conditions then, and it drew in large numbers and became an effective instrument of national activity. Though the contro and background were essentially middle class and city, it reached the remotest village and brought with it political and economic consciousness to the masses, and there was widespread discussion of national issues in city and village alike. One could feel the new life pulsating through this vast land of ours and, as we were in harmony with it, we drew strength from it. The intense repression by the Government during later years broke many of our physical and outward bonds with our countryside. But something more than that happened. The vague appeal of earlier days no longer sufficed, and on the new economic issues that were forcing themselves on us, we hesitated to give a definite opinion. Worse even than the physical divorce, there was a mental divorce between the middle-class elements and the mass elements. Our constitution no longer fitted in with changing conditions; it lost its roots in the soil and became a matter of small committees functioning in the air. It still had the mighty prestige of the Congress name behind it and this carried it a long way, but it had lost the living democratic touch. It became a prey to authoritarianism and a battleground for rival cliques fighting for control, and, in doing so, stooping to the lowest and most objectionable of tactics. Idealism disappeared, and in its place there came opportunism and corruption. The constitutional structure of the Congress was unequal to facing the new situation; it could be shaken up anywhere almost by a handful of unscrupulous individuals. Only a broad democratic basis could have saved it, and this was lacking.

Last year an attempt was made to revise the constitution in order to get rid of some of these evils. How far that attempt has succeeded or not I am not competent to judge. Perhaps it has made the organization more efficient, but efficiency means little if it has no strength behind it, and strength, for us, can only come from the masses. The present constitution stresses still further the authoritarian side of the organization, and in spite of stressing rural representation does not provide effective links with the masses.

The real problem for us is, how in our struggle for independence we can join together all the anti-imperialist forces in the country, how we can make a broad front of our mass elements with the great majority of the middle classes which stands for independence. There has been some talk of a joint front but, so far as I can gather, this refers to some alliance among the upper classes, probably at the expense of the masses. That surely can never be the idea of the Congress, and if it favours it it betrays the interests it has claimed to represent and loses the very reason for its existence. The essence of a joint popular front must be uncompromising opposition to imperialism, and the strength of it must inevitably come from the active participation of the peasantry and workers.

Perhaps you have wondered at the way I have dealt at some length with the background of international and national affairs and not touched so far the immediate problems that fill your minds. You may have grown impatient. But I am convinced that the only right way of looking at our own problems is to see them in their proper place in a world-setting. I am convinced that there is intimate connection between world events, and our national problem is but a part of the world problem of capitalist-imperialism. To look at each event apart from the others and without understanding the connection between them must lead to the formation of erratic and erroneous views. Look at the vast panorama of world change to-day, where mighty forces are at grips with each other and dreadful war darkens the horizon. Subject peoples struggling for freedom and imperialism crushing them down; exploited classes facing their exploiters and seeking freedom and equality. Italian imperialism bombing and killing the brave Ethiopians; Japanese imperialism continuing its aggression in North China and Mongolia; British imperialism piously objecting to other countries misbehaving, yet carrying on in much the same way in India and the Frontier; and behind it all a decaying economic order which intensifies all these conflicts. Can we not see an organic connection in all these various phenomena? Let us try to develop the historic sense so that we can view current events in proper perspective and understand their real significence. Only then can we appreciate the march of history and keep step with it.

I realize that in this address I am going a little beyond the usual beat of the Congress president. But I do not want you to have me under any false pretences, and we must have perfect frankness with each other. Most of you must know my views on social and economic matters, for I have often given expression to them. Yet you chose me as president. I do not take that choice to mean an endorsement by you all, or by a majority, of those views, but I take it that this does mean that those views are spreading in India and that most of you will be so indulgent as at least to consider them.

I am convinced that the only key to the solution of the world's problems and of India's problems lies in Socialism, and when I use this word I do so not in a vague humanitarian way but in the scientific, economic sense. Socialism is, however, something even more than an economic doctrine; it is a philosophy of life and as such also it appeals to me. I see no way of ending the poverty, the vast unemployment, the degradation, and the subjection of the Indian people except through Socialism. That involves vast and revolutionary changes in our political and social structure, the ending of vested interests in land and industry, as well as the feudal and autocratic Indian States system. That means the ending of private property, except in a restricted sense, and the replacement of the present profit system by a higher ideal of co-operative service. It means ultimately a change in our instincts and habits and desires. In short, it means a new civilization, radically different from the present capitalist order. Some glimpse we can have of this new civilization in the territories of the U.S.S.R. Much has happened there which has pained me greatly and with which I disagree, but I look upon that great and fascinating unfolding of a new order and a new civilization as the most promising feature of our dismal age. If the future is full of hope it is largely because of Soviet Russia and what it has done, and I am convinced that, if some world catastrophe does not intervene, this new civilization will spread to other lands and put an end to the wars and conflicts which capitalism feeds.

I do not know how or when this new order will come to India. I imagine that every country will fashion it after its own way and fit it in with its national genius. But the essential basis of that order must remain and be a link in the world order that will emerge out of the present chaos.

Socialism is thus for me not merely an economic doctrine which I favour; it is a vital creed which I hold with all my head and heart. I work for Indian independence because the nationalist in me cannot tolerate alien domination; I work for it even more because for me it is the inevitable step to social and economic change. I should like the Congress to become a Socialist organization and to join hands with the other forces in the world who are working for the new civilization. But I realize that the majority in the Congress, as it is constituted to-day, may not be prepared to go thus far. We are a nationalist organization, and we think and work on the nationalist plane. It is evident enough now that this is too narrow even for the limited objective of political independence, and so we talk of the masses and their economic needs. But still most of us hesitate, because of our nationalist backgrounds, to take a step which might frighten away some vested interests. Most of those interests are already ranged against us, and we can expect little from them except opposition even in the political struggle.

Much as I wish for the advancement of Socialism in this country, I have no desire to force the issue in the Congress and thereby create difficulties in the way of our struggle for independence. I shall co-operate gladly and with all the strength in me with all those who work for independence, even though they do not agree with the Socialist solution. But I shall do so stating my position frankly and hoping in course of time to convert the Congress and the country to it, for only thus can I see it achieving independence. It should surely be possible for all of us who believe in independence to join our ranks together even though we might differ on the social issue. The Congress has been in the past a broad front representing various opinions joined together by that common bond. It must continue as such even though the difference of those opinions becomes more marked.

How does Socialism fit in with the present ideology of the Congress? I do not think it does. I believe in the rapid industrialization of the country and only thus I think will the standards of the people rise substantially and poverty be combated. Yet I have co-operated wholeheartedly in the past with the khadi programme, and I hope to do so in the future because I believe that khadi and village industries have a definite place in our present economy. They have a social, a political, and an economic value which is difficult to measure but which is apparent enough to those who have studied their effects. But I look upon them more as temporary expedients of a transition stage rather than as solutions of our vital problems. That transition stage might be a long one, and in a country like India, village industries might well play an important, though subsidiary, role even after the development of industrialism. But though I co-operate in the village industries programme my ideological approach to it differs considerably from that of many others in the Congress who are opposed to industrialization and Socialism.

The problem of untouchability and the Harijans, again, can be approached in different ways. For a Socialist it presents no difficulty, for under Socialism there can be no such differentiation or victimization. Economically speaking, the Harijans have constituted the landless proletariat, and an economic solution removes the social barriers that custom and tradition have raised.

I come now to a question which is probably occupying your minds—the new Act passed by the British Parliament and our policy in regard to it. This Act has come into being since the last Congress met, but even at that time we had had a foretaste of it in the shape of the White Paper, and I know of no abler analysis of those provisions than that contained in the presidential address of my predecessor in this high office. The Congress rejected that proposed constitution, and resolved to have nothing to do with it. The new Act, as is well known, is an even more retrograde measure, and has been condemned by even the most moderate and cautious of our politicians. If we rejected the White Paper, what then are we to do with this new charter of slavery to strengthen the bonds of imperialist domination and to intensify the exploitation of our masses? And even if we forget its content for a while, can we forget the insult and injury that have accompanied it, the contemptuous defiance of our wishes, the suppression of civil liberties, and the widespread repression that has been our normal lot? If they had offered to us the crown of heaven with this accompaniment and with dishonour, would we not have spurned it as inconsistent with our national honour and self-respect? What, then, of this?

A charter of slavery is no law for the slave, and though we may perforce submit for a while to it and to the humiliation of ordinances and the like, inherent in that enforced submission is the right and the desire to rebel against it and to end it.

Our lawyers have examined this new constitution and have condemned it. But constitutions are something much more than legal documents. "The real constitution," said Ferdinand Lassalle, consists of "the actual relationships of power," and the working of this power we see even to-day, after the Act has been passed. That is the constitution we have to face, not the fine phrases which are sometimes presented to us, and we can only deal with it with the strength and power generated by the people of the country.

To this Act our attitude can only be one of uncompromising hostility and a constant endeavour to end it. How can we do this?

Since my return from Europe I have had the advantage of full and frank discussion with my colleagues of the Working Committee. All of us have agreed that the Act has to be rejected and combated, but all of us have not been able to agree to the manner of doing so. We have pulled together in the past and I earnestly hope that we shall do so in the future, but in order to do so effectively we must recognize that there are marked differences in our outlooks. I do not yet know, as I write, what the final recommendation of the Working Committee will be on this issue. I can only, therefore, venture to put before you my own personal views on the subject, not knowing how far they represent the views of Congressmen. I should like to make it clear, however, in fairness to my old colleagues of the Working Committee, that the majority of them do not agree with all the views I am going to express. But whether we agree or disagree, or whether we agree to differ, there is a strong desire on our part to continue to co-operate together, laying stress on our many points of agreement rather than on the differences. That is the right course for us and, as a democratic organization, that is the only course open to us.

I think that, under the circumstances, we have no choice but to contest the election to the new provincial legislatures in the event of their taking place. We should seek election on the basis of a detailed political and economic programme, with our demand for a Constituent Assembly in the forefront. I am convinced that the only solution of our political and communal problems will come through such an Assembly, provided it is elected on an adult franchise and a mass basis. That Assembly will not come into existence till at least a semi-revolutionary situation has been created in this country and the actual relationships of power, apart from paper constitutions, are such that the people of India can make their will felt. When that will happen I cannot say, but the world is too much in the grip of dynamic forces to-day to admit of static conditions in India or elsewhere for long. We may thus have to face this issue sooner than we might expect. But, obviously, a Constituent Assembly will not come through the new Act or the new legislatures. Yet we must press this demand and keep it before our country and the world, so that when the time comes we may be ripe for it.

A Constituent Assembly is the only proper and

democratic method for the framing of our constitution, and for its delegates then to negotiate a treaty with the representatives of the British Government. But we cannot go to it with blank minds in the hope that something good will emerge out of it. Such an Assembly, in order to be fruitful, must have previous thought behind it and a definite scheme put forward by an organized group. The actual details, as to how the Assembly is to be convened, must depend on the circumstances then existing and need not trouble us now. But it will be our function as the Congress to know exactly what we are after, to place this clearly and definitely before the Assembly, and to press for its acceptance.

One of the principal reasons for our seeking election will be to carry the message of the Congress to the millions of voters and to the scores of millions of the disfranchised, to acquaint them with our future programme and policy, to make the masses realize that we not only stand for them but that we are of them and seek to co-operate with them in removing their social and economic burdens. Our appeal and message will not be limited to the voters, for we must remember that hundreds of millions are disfranchised and they need our help most, for they are at the bottom of the social ladder and suffer most from exploitation. We have seen in the past widespread official interference in the elections; we shall have to face that, as well as the serried and monied ranks of the reactionaries. But the real danger will come from our toning down our programme and policy in order to win over the hesitating and compromising groups and individuals. If we compromise on principles, we shall fall between two stools and deserve our fall. The only right way and the only safe way is to stand four-square on our own programme and to compromise with no one who has opposed the national struggle for freedom in the past, or who is in any way giving support to British imperialism.

When we have survived the election, what then are we to do? Office or no office? A secondary matter, perhaps, and yet behind that issue lie deep questions of principle and vital differences of outlook, and a decision on that, either way, has far-reaching consequences. Behind it lies, somewhat hidden, the question of independence itself and whether we seek revolutionary changes in India or are working for petty reforms under the aegis of British imperialism. We go back again in thought to the clash of ideas which preceded the changes in the Congress in 1920. We made a choice then deliberately and with determination, and discarded the old sterile creed of reformism. Are we to go back again to that blind and suffocating lane, after all these years of brave endeavour, and to wipe out the memory of what we have done and achieved and suffered? That is the issue, and let none of us forget it when we have to give our decision. In this India, crying aloud for radical and fundamental change, in this world pregnant with revolutionary and dynamic possibility, are we to forget our mission and our historic destiny, and slide back to static futility? And if some of us feel tired and hunger for rest and quiet, do we imagine that India's masses will follow our lead, when elemental forces and economic necessity are driving them to their inevitable goal? If we enter the back-waters, others will take our place on the bosom of the flowing stream and will dare to take the rapids and ride the torrent.

How has this question arisen? If we express our hostility to the Act and reject the entire scheme, does it not follow logically that we should have nothing to do with the working of it and should prevent its functioning, in so far as we can? To accept office and ministry, under the conditions of the Act, is to negative our rejection of it and to stand self-condemned. National honour and self-respect cannot accept this position, for it would inevitably mean our co-operation in some measure with the repressive apparatus of imperialism, and we would become partners in this repression and in the exploitation of our people. Of course, we would try to champion the rights of the people and would protest against repression, but as ministers under the Act, we could do very little to give relief, and we would have to share responsibility for the administration with the apparatus of imperialism, for the deficit budgets, for the suppression of labour and the peasantry. It is always dangerous to assume responsibility without power, even in democratic countries; it will be far worse with this undemocratic constitution, hedged in with safeguards and reserved powers and mortgaged funds, where we have to follow the rules and regulations of our opponents' making. Imperialism sometimes talks of co-operation, but the kind of co-operation it wants is usually known as surrender, and the ministers who accept office will have to do so at the price of surrender of much that they might have stood for in public. That is a humiliating position which self-respect itself should prevent one from accepting. For our great national organization to be party to it is to give up the very basis and background of our existence.

Self-respect apart, common sense tells us that we can lose much and gain little by acceptance of office in terms of the Act. We cannot get much out of it, or else our criticism of the Act itself is wrong, and we know that it is not so. The big things for which we stand will fade into the background and petty issues will absorb our attention, and we shall lose ourselves in compromises and communal tangles, and disillusion with us will spread over the land. If we have a majority, and only then can the question of acceptance of office arise, we shall be in a position to dominate the situation and to prevent reactionaries and imperialists from profiting by it. Office will not add to our real strength, it will only weaken us by making us responsible for many things that we utterly dislike.

Again, if we are in a minority, the question of office does not arise. It may be, however, that we are on the verge of a majority and with the co-operation of other individuals and groups we can obtain office. There is nothing inherently wrong in our acting together with others on specific issues of civil liberty or economic or other demands, provided we do not compromise on any principle. But I can imagine few things more dangerous and more likely to injure us than the acceptance of office on the sufferance of others. That would be an intolerable position.

It is said that our chances at the elections would increase if we announced that we were prepared to accept offices and ministries. Perhaps that might be so, for all manner of other people, eager for the spoils and patronage that office gives, would then hurry to join us. Does any Congressman imagine that this would be a desirable development or that we would gain strength thereby? Again it is said that more voters would vote for us if they knew that we were going to form ministries. That might happen if we deluded them with false promises of what we might do for them within the Act, but a quick nemesis would follow our failure to give effect to those promises, and failure would be inevitable if the promises were worth while.

There is only one straight course open to us, to go to the people with our programme and make it clear to them that we cannot give effect to the major items in it under present conditions, and therefore, while we use the platform of the legislatures to press that programme, we seek to end these imperialist bodies by creating deadlocks in them whenever we are in a position to do so. Those deadlocks should preferably take place on those programmes so that the masses might learn how ineffective for their purposes are these legislatures.

One fact is sometimes forgotten—the provision for second chambers in many of the provinces. These chambers will be reactionary and will be exploited by the Governor to check any forward tendencies in the lower house. They will make the position of a minister, who seeks advance, even more difficult and unenviable.

Some people have suggested, though their voices are hushed now, that provincial autonomy might be given on this office issue and each Provincial Congress Committee should be empowered to decide it for its own province. An astonishing and fatal suggestion playing into the hands of our imperialist rulers. We who have laboured for Indian unity can never be parties to any proposal which tends to lessen that unity. That way lies disaster and a disruption of the forces working for freedom. If we agree to this, why then should we also not agree to the communal issue being decided provincially, or many other issues, where individual provinces might think differently? First issues will sink into the background, independence itself will fade away, and the narrowest provincialism raise its ugly head. Our policy must be uniform for the whole of India, and it must place first things first, and independence is the first thing of all.

So that I am convinced that for the Congress to favour the acceptance of office, or even to hesitate and waver about it, would be a vital error. It will be a pit from which it would be difficult for us to come out. Practical statesmanship is against it, as well as the traditions of the Congress and the mentality we have sought to develop in the people. Psychologically, any such lead might have disastrous consequences. If we stand for revolutionary changes, as we do, we have to cultivate a revolutionary mentality among our people, and anything that goes against it is harmful to our cause.

This psychological aspect is important. For we must never forget, and never delude our masses into imagining that we can get any real power or real freedom through working these legislatures. We may use them certainly to advance our cause to some extent, but the burden of the struggle for freedom must fall on the masses, and primarily, therefore, our effective work must lie outside these legislatures. Strength will come from the masses and from our work among them and our organization of them.

Of secondary importance though the work in the legislatures is, we may not treat it casually and allow it to become a hindrance to our other work. Therefore it is necessary for the Congress, through its executive, to have direct control over the elections and the programme placed before the country, as well as the activity in the legislatures. Such control will inevitably be exercised through committees and boards appointed for the purpose, but the continued existence of semi-autonomous parliamentary boards seems to be undesirable. Provision should also be made for a periodical review of all such activities, so that Congressmen in general and the country should keep in touch with them and should influence them.

We have considered the provincial elections which, it is said, may take place early next year. The time is far off yet, and it is by no means impossible that these elections may not take place for a much longer time, or may not take place at all, and the new Act may take its rightful place in oblivion. Much may happen in the course of the next year, and war is ever on the horizon, to upset the schemes and time-tables of our rulers. But we cannot speculate on this, and we have to make provision for contingencies. That decision might even have been delayed, but dangerous and compromising tendencies seek to influence Congress policy, and the Congress cannot remain silent when the issue is raised and its whole future is in the balance.

The provincial legislatures may come, but few persons, I imagine, are confident about the coming of the federal part of this unholy structure. So far as we are concerned, we shall fight against it to our utmost strength, and the primary object of our creating deadlocks in the provinces and making the new Act difficult of functioning, is to kill the Federation. With the Federation dead, the provincial end of the Act will also go and leave the slate clean for the people of India to write on. That writing, whatever it be, can never admit the right of the Indian States to continue as feudal and autocratic monarchies. They have long survived their day, propped up by an alien Power, and have become the strangest anomalies in a changing world. The future has no place for autocracy or feudalism; a free India cannot tolerate the subjection of many of her children and their deprivation of human rights, nor can it ever agree to a dissection of its body and a cutting up of its limbs. If we stand for any human, political, social, or economic rights for ourselves, we stand for those identical rights for the people of the States.

I have referred to the terrible suppression of civil liberties by the British Government in India. But in the States matters are even worse, and though we know that the real power behind those States is that of British imperialism, this tragic suppression of our brothers by their own countrymen is of painful significance. Indian Rulers and their ministers have spoken and acted increasingly in the approved Fascist manner, and their record during the past few years especially has been one of aggressive opposition to our national demands. States which are considered advanced ban the Congress organization and offer insult to our national flag, and decree new laws to suppress the Press. What shall we say of the more backward and primitive States?

There is one more matter concerning the Constitution Act which has given rise to much controversy. This is the communal decision. Many people have condemned it strongly and, I think, rightly; few have a good word for it. My own viewpoint is, however, somewhat different from that of others. I am not concerned so much with what it gives to this group or that, but more so with the basic idea behind it. It seeks to divide India into numerous separate compartments, chiefly on a religious basis, and thus makes the development of democracy and economic policy very difficult. Indeed the communal decision and democracy can never go together. We have to admit that, under present circumstances, and so long as our policies are dominated by middle-class elements, we cannot do away with communalism altogether. But to make a necessary exception in favour of our Muslim or Sikh friends is one thing, to spread this evil principle to numerous other groups and thus to divide up the electoral machinery and the legislature into many compartments, is a far more dangerous proposition. If we wish to function democratically the proposed communal arrangement will have to go, and I have no doubt that it will go. But it will not go by the methods adopted by the aggressive opponents of the decision. These methods result inevitably in perpetuating the decision, for they help in continuing a situation which prevents any reconsideration.

I have not been enamoured of the past Congress policy in regard to the communal question and its attempts to make pacts and compromises. Yet essentially I think it was based on a sound instinct. First of all the Congress always put independence first and other questions, including the communal one, second, and refused to allow any of those other questions to take pride of place. Secondly, it argued that the communal problem had arisen from a certain set of circumstances which enabled the third party to exploit the other two. In order to solve it, one had either to get rid of the third party (and that means independence), or get rid of that set of circumstances, which meant a friendly approach by the parties concerned and an attempt to soften the prejudice and fear that filled them. Thirdly, that the majority community must show generosity in the matter to allay the fear and suspicion that minorities, even though unreasonably, might have.

That analysis is, I think, perfectly sound. I would add that, in my opinion, a real solution of the problem will only come when economic issues, affecting all religious groups and cutting across communal boundaries, arise. Apart from the upper middle classes, who live in hopes of office and patronage, the masses and the lower middle classes have to face identical political and economic problems. It is odd and significant that all the communal demands of any group, of which so much is heard, have nothing whatever to do with these problems of the masses and the lower middle classes.

It is also significant that the principal communal leaders, Hindu or Moslem or others, are political reactionaries, quite apart from the communal question. It is sad to think how they have sided with British imperialism in vital matters, how they have given their approval to the suppression of civil liberty, how during these years of agony they have sought to gain narrow profit for their group at the expense of the larger cause of freedom. With them there can be no co-operation, for that would mean co-operation with reaction. But I am sure that with the larger masses and the middle classes, who may have temporarily been led away by the specious claims of their communal leaders, there must be the fullest co-operation, and out of that co-operation will come a fairer solution of this problem.

I am afraid I cannot get excited over this communal issue, important as it is temporarily. It is after all a side issue, and it can have no real importance in the larger scheme of things. Those who think of it as the major issue, think in terms of British imperialism continuing permanently in this country. Without that basis of thought, they would not attach so much importance to one of its inevitable offshoots. I have no such fear, and so my vision of a future India contains neither imperialism nor communalism.

Yet the present difficulty remains and has to be faced. Especially our sympathy must go to the people of Bengal who have suffered most from these communal decisions, as well as from the heavy hand of the Government. Whenever opportunity offers to improve their situation in a friendly way, we must seize it. But always the background of our action must be the national struggle for independence and the social freedom of the masses.

I have referred previously to the growing divorce between our organization and the masses. Individually many of us still have influence with the masses and our word carries weight with them, and who can measure the love and reverence of India's millions for our leader, Gandhiji? And yet organizationally we have lost that intimate touch that we had. The social reform activities of the khadi and village industries and Harijan organizations keep large numbers of our comrades in touch with the masses and those contacts bear fruit. But they are essentially non-political and so, politically, we have largely lost touch. There are many reasons for this and some are beyond our control. Our present Congress constitution is, I feel, not helpful in developing these contacts or in encouraging enough the democratic spirit in its primary committees. These committees are practically rolls of voters who meet only to elect delegates or representatives, and take no part in discussion or the formation of policy.

It is interesting to read in that monumental and impressive record, the Webbs' new book on Russia, how the whole Soviet structure is based on a wide and living democratic foundation. Russia is not supposed to be a democratic country after the Western pattern, and yet we find the essentials of democracy present in far greater degree amongst the masses there than anywhere else. The six hundred thousand towns and villages there have a vast democratic organization, each with its own soviet, constantly discussing, debating, criticizing, helping in the formulation of policy, electing representatives to higher committees. This organization as citizens covers the entire population over eighteen years of age. There is yet another vast organization of the people as producers, and a third, equally vast, as consumers. And thus scores of millions of men and women are constantly taking part in the discussion of public affairs, and actually in the administration of the country. There has been no such practical application of the democratic process in history.

All this is, of course, utterly beyond us, for it requires a change in the political and economic structure and much else before we can experiment that way. But we can profit by that example still, and try in our own limited way to develop democracy in the lowest rungs of the Congress ladder and make the primary committee a living organization.

An additional method for us to increase our contacts with the masses is to organize them as producers and then affiliate such organizations to the Congress or have full co-operation between the two. Such organizations of producers as exist to-day, such as trade unions and peasant unions, as well as other anti-imperialist organizations could also be brought within this sphere of mutual co-operation for the good of the masses and for the struggle for national freedom. Thus Congress could have an individual as well as a corporate membership, and retaining its individual character, could influence, and be influenced by, other mass elements.

These are big changes that I have hinted at, and I am by no means sure how they can be brought about, or whether it is possible to go far in this direction in the near future. Still we must move to some extent, at least, if we are to have our roots in the soil of India and draw life and strength from its millions. The subject is fascinating but complicated and can only be tackled by an expert committee which I trust will be appointed on behalf of the Congress. The report of that committee must be freely discussed so as to get the widest backing for it.

All this will take us to the next Congress. Meanwhile, perhaps, some urgent changes are needed in our constitution to remove anomalies and avoid difficulties. Owing to my absence I have had little experience of the working of the new constitution, and cannot make any concrete suggestions. The reduction in the numbers of delegates and All-India Congress Committee members would be, to some extent, desirable if there was a background of widespread activity in the primary and secondary committees. Without it, it makes us even less responsive to mass opinion, and, therefore, an increase seems desirable. But the real solution is to increase the interest and day-to-day activity of the lower committees.

I have been told that the manual labour franchise has not been a success, and has led to a great deal of evasion. If that is so a change is desirable, for a constitution must be such as can be worked easily and without subterfuge.

The Congress is an all-inclusive body and represents many interests, but essentially it is a political organization with various subsidiary and allied organizations, like the Spinners' Association and the Village Industries Association. These allied organizations work in the economic field, but they do not seek directly to remove the burdens of the peasantry under the present system of land tenure. Nor can the Congress, situated as it is, wholly function as a peasant organization, although in many provinces it has espoused the cause of the peasantry and brought them much relief. It seems to me necessary that the Congress should encourage the formation of peasant unions as well as workers' unions, and co-operate with such as already exist, so that the day-to-day struggle of the masses might be carried on on the basis of their economic demands and other grievances.[*] This identification of the Congress with the economic struggle of the masses will bring us nearer to them and nearer to freedom than anything else. I would welcome also the organization of other special interests, like those of the women, in the general framework of our national struggle for freedom. The

Congress would be in a position to co-ordinate all these vital activities and thus to base itself on the widest possible mass foundation.

There has been some talk of a militant programme and militant action. I do not know what exactly is meant, but if direct action on a national scale or civil disobedience are meant, then I would say that I see no near prospect of them. Let us not indulge in tall talk before we are ready for big action. Our business to-day is to put our house in order, to sweep away the defeatist mentality of some people, and to build up our organization with its mass affiliations, as well as to work amongst the masses. The time may come, and that sooner perhaps than we expect, when we might be put to the test. Let us get ready for that test. Civil disobedience and the like cannot be switched on and off when we feel like doing so. It depends on many things, some of which are beyond our control, but in these days of revolutionary change and constantly recurring crises in the world, events often move faster than we do. We shall not lack for opportunities.

The major problem of India to-day is that of the land—of rural poverty and unemployment and a thoroughly out-of-date land system. A curious combination of circumstances has held back India during the past few generations, and the political and economic garments it wears no longer fit it and are torn and tattered. In some ways our agrarian conditions are not unlike those of France a hundred and fifty years ago, prior to the great revolution. They cannot continue so for long. At the same time we have become part of international capitalism and we suffer the pains and crises which afflict this decaying system. As a result of these elemental urges and conflicts of world forces what will emerge in India none can say. But we can say with confidence that the present order has reached the evening of its day, and it is up to us to try to mould the future as we would like it to be.

The world is filled with rumours and alarms of war. In Abyssinia bloody and cruel war has already gone on for many months, and we have watched anew how hungry and predatory imperialism behaves in its mad search for colonial domains. We have watched also with admiration the brave fight of the Ethiopians for their freedom against heavy odds. You will permit me, I feel sure, to greet them on your behalf and express our deep sympathy for them. Their struggle is something more than a local struggle. It is one of the first effective checks by an African people on an advancing imperialism, and already it has had far-reaching consequences.

In the Far East, also, war hovers on the horizon, and we see an Eastern imperialism advancing methodically and pitilessly over ancient China and dreaming of world empire. Imperialism shows its claws wherever it may be, in the West or in the East.

In Europe an aggressive Fascism or Naziism steps continuously on the brink of war and vast armed camps arise in preparation for what seems to be the inevitable end of all this. Nations join hands to fight other nations, and progressive forces in each country ally themselves to fight the Fascist menace.

Where do we come in in this awful game? What

part shall we play in this approaching tragedy? It is difficult to say. But we must not permit ourselves to be passive tools exploited for imperialist ends. It must be our right to say whether we join a war or not, and without that consent there should be no co-operation from us. When the time comes we may have little say in the matter, and so it becomes necessary for the Congress to declare clearly now its opposition to India's participation in any imperialist war, and every war that will be waged by imperialist Powers will be an imperialist war, whatever the excuses put forward might be. Therefore we must keep out of it and not allow Indian lives and Indian money to be sacrificed.

To the progressive forces of the world, to those who stand for human freedom and the breaking of political and social bonds, we offer our full co-operation in their struggle against imperialism and Fascist reaction, for we realize that our struggle is a common one. Our grievance is not against any people or any country as such, and we know that even in imperialist England, which throttles us, there are many who do not love imperialism and who stand for freedom.

During this period of difficulty and storm and stress, inevitably our minds and hearts turn to our great leader who has guided us and inspired us by his dynamic personality these many years. Physical ill-health prevents him now from taking his full share in public activities. Our good wishes go out to him for his rapid and complete recovery, and with those wishes is the selfish desire to have him back again amongst us. We have differed from him in the past and we shall differ from him in the future about many things, and it is right that each one of us should act up to his convictions. But the bonds that hold us together are stronger and more vital than our differences, and the pledges we took together still ring in our ears. How many of us have that passionate desire for Indian independence and the raising of our poverty-stricken masses which consumes him? Many things he taught us long years ago it seems now—fearlessness and discipline, and the will to sacrifice ourselves for the larger cause. That lesson may have grown dim but we have not forgotten it, nor can we ever forget him who has made us what we are and raised India again from the depths. The pledge of independence that we took together still remains to be redeemed, and we await again for him to guide us with his wise counsel.

But no leader, however great he be, can shoulder the burden single-handed; we must all share it to the best of our ability and not seek helplessly to rely on others to perform miracles. Leaders come and go; many of our best-loved captains and comrades have left us all too soon, but India goes on and so does India's struggle for freedom. It may be that many of us must suffer still and die so that India may live and be free. The promised land may yet be far from us, and we may have to march wearily through the deserts, but who will take away from us that deathless hope which has survived the scaffold and immeasurable suffering and sorrow; who will dare to crush the spirit of India which has found rebirth again and again after so many crucifixions?

4

PRISON-LAND*

A WRITER in a recent issue of an English periodical stated that the stress and strain of politics and prison life had broken me up. I do not know what his sources of information were, but I can say from a fairly intimate knowledge of my body and mind, that both of them are tough and sound and not in any danger of a break-up or collapse in the near future. Fortunately for myself, I have always attached importance to bodily health and physical fitness, and though I have often enough ill-treated my body, I have seldom permitted it to fall ill. Mental health is a more invisible commodity, but I have taken sufficient care of that also and I am vain enough to imagine that I possess more of it than many a person who has not had to suffer the strain of active Congress politics and passive gaol life.

But my health or ill-health is a small matter which need not worry anyone, although friends and newspapers have given it undue prominence. What is far more important, from the national and social point of view, is the state of the prisons and the bodily and mental conditions of the vast population that they house in India. It is a notorious fact that strong and brave men have suffered greatly and even collapsed bodily under the terrible strain of prolonged gaol life

* First published in Allahabad, 1934.

and detention. I have seen my nearest and dearest suffer in prison and the list of my personal friends who have done so is a long and painful one. Only recently a dear and valued colleague, a friend whom I first met in Cambridge more than a quarter of a century ago, and who was among the bravest of the brave in this unhappy country of ours, J. M. Sen-Gupta,* met his death while under detention.

It is natural that we should feel the sufferings of our colleagues, and those whom we have known, more than the misery of the thousands who are unknown to us. And yet it is not about them that I am writing these few lines. We, who have willingly sought to pass the forbidding iron gates of prison, have no wish to squeal or to complain of the treatment given. If any of our countrymen are interested and wish to raise the question, it is for them to do so. Such questions are frequently raised, but as a rule they relate to well-known individuals, and special treatment for them is sought on the ground of their social position. To meet the clamour, a small handful are given what is called "A" and "B" class treatment; the great majority, probably over 95 per cent, face the full rigours of gaol life.

This differentiation into various classes has often been criticized and rightly criticized. To a slight extent it might be justified on medical grounds, for it is highly probable that some people, used to a different diet, may develop the most violent disorders, as indeed

* One of the chief Congress leaders in Bengal. He died largely as a result of imprisonment in 1934, when only in the early forties.

many do, if they have to subsist on gaol diet. It is also obvious that some persons are physically incapable of the extreme forms of manual labour. But, apart from this, it is a little difficult to imagine the justification for depriving "C" class prisoners of the so-called privileges given to others. A higher class is supposed to be given because of higher "social status" or a higher standard of life. One of the tests laid down, I believe, is the amount of land revenue a person pays. Does it follow from a higher revenue that the person is more attached to his family and is therefore entitled to more interviews or letters? Or that greater facilities should be given for reading and writing? Those who pay large sums as land revenue are not usually noted for their intellectual attainments.

I do not, of course, mean to imply that those who get special facilities for interviews or letters or reading and writing should be deprived of these. These so-called privileges are poor enough as they stand, and it is well to realize that in most other countries the worst and lowest type of prisoner gets far more "privileges" of this kind than even the "A" class prisoner in India. And yet these "A" and "B" class privileges are given to such an insignificant number that they might well be ignored in considering the Indian prison system. Fundamentally, "A" and "B" classes are meant as something to show off and soothe public opinion. Most people who do not know the real facts are misled by them.

Some of the "A" class prisoners, as also especially some of the detenus or State prisoners, have often to undergo one experience which is peculiarly distressing.

They are kept alone without a companion for many months at a time, and, as every doctor knows, this loneliness is very bad for the average person. Only those who have strictly trained and disciplined their minds and can turn inwards can escape ill effects. It is true that the prisoner or detenu is given the advantage of a few minutes' conversation daily with a member of the prison staff, but this is an advantage which is not seized with cheering and acclamation. This policy of more or less solitary confinement is apparently quite deliberate on the part of Government. I remember that about the time I was arrested in December 1931, Khan Abdul Ghaffar Khan* was also arrested in Peshawar or Charsadda. Four arrests were made at the same time: Khan Abdul Ghaffar Khan, his brother Dr. Khan Sahib, Dr. Khan Sahib's young son, and a colleague of theirs. They were all brought down by special train and distributed in four separate prisons in four different cities. It was easy enough to keep all of them, or father and son, or brothers together. But this was deliberately avoided and each one was, I believe, kept alone by himself without any companion. At any rate I know that Dr. Khan Sahib was so kept in Naini prison. For over a month I was also in Naini then, but we were kept apart and not allowed to meet. It was tantalizing for me, for Dr. Khan Sahib was a dear friend of my student days in England and I had not met him for many years.

* The leader of the Puritan Revolution, the "Khudai Khitmatgars," or Servants of God, among the men of the North-West Frontier.

It is not a question of favoured treatment for political prisoners. I know perfectly well that the treatment of politicals will grow progressively worse, as it has done in the course of the last dozen years. The only possible check is that of public opinion, but even that does not count in the last resort unless it is so strong as to ensure victory.

Thus it is obvious that political prisoners must expect progressively bad treatment. In 1930–1 the treatment was worse than in 1921–2, in 1932 it was worse than in 1930–1. To-day an ordinary political prisoner is certainly worse off in gaol than a non-political convict. Every effort is often made to harass him into apologizing or at least to make him thoroughly frightened of prison.

It has been stated on behalf of Sir Samuel Hoare in the House of Commons that "over 500 persons in India were whipped during 1932 for offences in connection with the civil disobedience movement." The existence or otherwise of whipping is often considered a test of the degree of civilization in a State. Many advanced States have done away with it altogether, and even where it has been retained it has been kept for what are considered the most degrading and brutal crimes, such as violent rape on immature girls. Some months ago, I believe, there was a discussion in the Assembly on the question of retaining the punishment of whipping for certain (non-political) crimes. It was pointed out by Government spokesmen that this was necessary for some brutal crimes. Probably every psychologist and psychiatrist is of a contrary opinion and holds that a brutal punishment is the most foolish of methods for dealing with brutal crimes. But, however that may be, in India we see that it is quite a common occurrence now for flogging to be administered for purely political and technical offences, admittedly involving no moral turpitude, or for petty offences against prison discipline.

Yet another advance has been recorded in the treatment of women political prisoners. Many hundreds of women were sentenced and an extraordinarily small number of them were put in "A" or "B" classes. As it happens, the lot of women in prison—political or non-political—is far worse than that of men. Men do move about within the gaol in going to and fro in connection with their work; they have change and movement and this is helpful in refreshing their minds to some extent. Women, though given lighter work, are closely confined in a small place and lead a terribly monotonous existence. Women convicts are also as a rule far worse as companions than the average male convicts. Among men there is a large proportion of thoroughly non-criminal types, decent village folk who had a brawl over a land dispute and managed to get long sentences as a result. The criminal element is proportionately much higher among the women. The great majority of women political prisoners, most of them bright young girls, had to endure this suffocating atmosphere. It seems to me that hardly anything that has taken place in our prisons or outside is quite so bad as the treatment of our women folk.

I would not have any woman, whether she belongs

to the middle classes or the peasantry or the working classes, subjected to the treatment that has been accorded to them in our prisons. As it happens, the great majority of women political prisoners have been from the bourgeois or middle classes. The peasant may go to prison for a political purpose but his wife goes very seldom. Considered from the standpoint of Government, the social standards of the women politicals were relatively high.

In the course of a speech in the United Provinces Legislative Council last year, the then Home Member made the flesh of members creep by suggesting that if conditions in gaols were improved for politicals, all the dacoits would forthwith come to gaol as political prisoners. I believe he advanced some similar argument against improving the conditions of women prisoners. No doubt these arguments were up to the intellectual standards of the majority of his audience and they served their purpose. For those of us who live in the outer darkness, it is interesting to plumb the depths of knowledge and understanding which the Home Member's statement revealed—understanding of the nature of dacoits and the like, knowledge of criminology, psychology, and human nature. The arguments lead us to certain conclusions which perhaps did not occur to the Home Member. If a dacoit is prepared to leave his profession and go to gaol, if gaol is not too harsh, it follows that he will be much more prepared to quit dacoity and crime if a minimum of security and life's necessaries come to him outside gaol. That is, the urge to dacoity is the economic urge of hunger and distress; remove this urge and dacoity goes. The cure for dacoity and crime is thus not heavy punishment but removal of the basic cause. But I have no desire to make last year's Home Member responsible for such far-reaching and revolutionary notions, although they may logically follow from what he said. From another and a higher office he has been letting us have occasional glimpses of his deep knowledge of the laws of economics and no doubt he would repudiate such heresy.

Reference is often made to political prisoners and Government has refused to classify them separately. I think, under the circumstances, Government has been right. For who are the politicals? It is easy enough to separate the civil disobedience prisoners, but there are many other ways of catching an inconvenient political agitator than under the so-called political sections of various laws and ordinances. It is a common occurrence in rural areas for peasant leaders and workers to be run in under the preventive sections of the Criminal Procedure Code or even for more serious offences. Such persons are as much political prisoners as any others and there are large numbers of them. This procedure is not usual in the larger towns because of the publicity involved.

High walls and iron gates cut off the little world of prison from the wide world outside. Here in this prison world everything is different; there are no colours, no changes, no movement, no hope, no joy for the long-term prisoner, the "lifer." Life runs its dull round with a terrible monotony; it is all flat desert land with no high points and no oases to quench one's thirst or shelter one from the burning heat. Days run into weeks, and weeks into months and years till the sands of life run out.

All the might of the State is against him and none of the ordinary checks are available. Even the voice of pain is hushed, the cry of agony cannot be heard beyond the high walls. In theory there are some checks and visitors and officials from outside go to inspect. But it is rare for a prisoner to dare to complain to them, and those who dare have to suffer for their daring. The visitor goes, the petty gaol officials remain, and it is with them that he has to pass his days. It is not surprising that he prefers to put up with his troubles rather than risk an addition to them.

The coming of political prisoners in large numbers threw some light into the dark corners of prison-land. A breath of fresh air came in bringing with it some hope to the long-term prisoner. Public opinion was stirred a little and some improvements followed. But they were few and essentially the system remains as it was. Sometimes one hears of "riots" in gaols. What exactly does this signify? Perhaps the prisoners were to blame. And yet it is a mad thing for unarmed, helpless prisoners, surrounded by high walls, to challenge the armed might of the gaol staff. There can only be one outcome of it, and inevitably one is led to think that only extreme provocation could induce the prisoners to this act of folly and despair.

There are inquiries, either departmental or perhaps by the District Magistrate. What chance has the prisoner? On the one side a fully prepared case supported by the staff and the numerous prisoners who must do their bidding; on the other, a frightened shivering outcaste of humanity, manacled and fettered, who has no one's sympathy and whom no one believes. The Judicial Secretary to the United Provinces Government stated in the local Council last November that those who had been confined in gaol, being interested parties, must be considered as unreliable. So the poor prisoner being very much an interested party when he is himself beaten or ill-treated cannot obviously be believed. It would be interesting to find out from the United Provinces Government what evidence, short of the testimony of the invisible and supernatural powers, a prisoner could produce under the circumstances.

But for the tragedy behind them one might appreciate the humour of private governmental inquiries. Sir Samuel Hoare grows righteously indignant whenever any charge is made against the police or the gaol staffs and is consistent in refusing all public or impartial inquiries. I seem to recollect that there was a departmental inquiry in the Hijli* affair about two years ago, and shortly afterwards an official inquiry held that the official version of the occurrences had been entirely wrong. But then that was an unusual affair. Most departmental inquiries are not checked in this way. One feels like having recourse to the delightful plays

* Hijli is a place in Bengal where there is an "internment camp" for detenus—i.e. inhabitants of Bengal who have been either convicted or suspected of terrorism or of connections with it.

of Sir William Gilbert for an analogy, or perhaps that classic of English childhood, the immortal Alice, is even more suitable:

> Fury said to a mouse,
> That he found in the house,
> "Let us both go to law:
> I will prosecute you.
> We must have the trial;
> For really this morning
> I've nothing to do!"
> Said the mouse to the cur,
> "Such a trial, dear sir,
> With no jury or judge,
> Would be wasting your breath."
> "I'll be judge, I'll be jury,"
> Said cunning old Fury;
> "I'll try the whole cause
> And condemn you to death."

I had a personal experience last year which has a certain wider significance. The jailor of the Allahabad District Jail insulted and hustled out my mother and wife when they were having an interview with my brother-in-law. I was angry when I heard this. And yet I did not attach much importance to the incident for all it signified was that an ill-trained and ill-mannered official had misbehaved. I expected some expression of regret from some higher official. Instead, punishments were awarded by Government to my mother, wife, and brother-in-law, of course without the slightest reference to them. Indirectly I was punished by not being allowed to see my mother or wife for a period. An inquiry from me to the

Inspector-General brought a brief reply containing an unmannerly reference to my mother. It was only at this stage that Government found out the true facts from me and from statements made by my mother and wife.

It was obvious that they had erred egregiously. In spite of my asking them repeatedly they have not pointed out any error in our statements and I must therefore take it that they accept those versions, as indeed they must. If so, they had acted very foolishly in the first instance and the least they could do was to express regret. I am still waiting for that straightforward expression of regret.

If such treatment can be accorded to my mother and wife and can be followed by the strange behaviour and obstinacy of Government, it can well be imagined what the average less-known prisoner and his people have to put up with. Our whole system of government, superimposed as it is from above and without any roots in the people, can only hang together so long as one peg supports the other. That is its strength, and that, fortunately, is its weakness, for where the collapse of such a system comes, it is complete.

Last year I ventured to write to the Home Member from prison and I told him that after twelve years of a fairly extended experience of prison conditions in the United Provinces, I had come very regretfully to the conclusion that the gaols in this province were steeped in corruption and violence and falsehood. Many years ago I pointed out some of the abuses to a Superintendent of my prison (he became Inspector-

General afterwards). He admitted them and said that when he first joined the Prison Department he was full of enthusiasm for reform. Later he found that little could be done, so he allowed things to take their course.

Indeed little can be done by the best of individuals—and many of those in charge can hardly be considered shining examples. An Indian prison is after all a replica of the larger India. What counts is the objective—is it human welfare or just the working of a machine or the preservation of vested interests? Why are punishments given—as society's or Government's revenge or with the object of reforming?

Do judges or prison officers ever think that the unhappy wretch before them should be made into a person capable of filling his place in society when he comes out of prison? It almost seems an impertinence to raise these questions, for how many people really care?

Our judges are, let us hope, large-hearted; they are certainly long-sentencing. Here is an Associated Press message from Peshawar dated December 15, 1932: "For writing threatening letters to the Inspector-General of Police and other high officials of the Frontier soon after the Coldstream murder, accused named Jamnadas has been sentenced by the City Magistrate of Peshawar to eight years' imprisonment under Section 500–507 I.P.C." Jamnadas was apparently a young boy.

Here is another remarkable instance—also an Associated Press message, dated April 22, 1933, from Lahore: "For being in possession of a knife with a blade seven inches long, a young Muslim named Saadat was sentenced by the City Magistrate under Section 19 of the Arms Act to eighteen months' rigorous imprisonment."

And a third instance from Madras, dated July 6, 1933. A boy named Ramaswami threw a harmless cracker in the court of the Chief Presidency Magistrate as he was engaged in a conspiracy case hearing. Ramaswami was sentenced to four years, apparently in a Juvenile Prison.

These are three not unusual instances. They could easily be multiplied and there are worse cases. I suppose people are long-suffering in India and past all astonishment at such amazing sentences. Personally I find that no amount of practice can prevent my gasping when I read of them. Anywhere else, except in Nazi Germany, such sentences would create a tremendous outcry.

And justice is not entirely blind in India; it keeps one eye open. In every agrarian brawl or riot large numbers of peasants get life sentences. Usually these petty riots take place when an exasperated tenantry are goaded beyond endurance by the agents of the landlords. A simple process of identifying all those who are supposed to have been present on the scene is enough to condemn them for life or to long terms of imprisonment. Hardly any attention is paid to the provocation and even the identification is usually of the feeblest kind. It is easy to drag in any individual who is in the bad books of the police. If the affair can be given a political tinge or connected with a no-rent campaign a conviction is all the easier and the sentences the heavier.

In a recent case a peasant who slapped a tax-collector was awarded a year's imprisonment. Another instance is somewhat different. It took place last July in Meerut. A Naib Tahsildar* went to realize irrigation dues from the residents of a village One peasant was carried by the peons to where the Naib was seated and the peons complained that this man's wife and son had beaten them. A somewhat remarkable story. However, the Naib ordered that the peasant should be vicariously punished for his wife's offence and the three of them, the Naib and the two peons, beat the unhappy man with sticks. As a result of the beating the man died later. The Naib and the peons were subsequently tried and convicted for simple hurt but they were forthwith released on probation of good conduct for six months. The good conduct, I suppose, signified that they must not beat another man to death within the next six months. The comparison of these cases is instructive.

So the question of prison reform leads us inevitably to a reform of our criminal procedure and, even more so, a reform in the mentalities of our judges who still think in terms of a hundred years ago and are blissfully ignorant of modern ideas of punishment and reform. That of course leads, as everything else does, to a change of the whole system of government.

But to confine ourselves to the prisons. Any reform must be based on the idea that a prisoner is not punished but reformed and made into a good citizen. (I am of

* A local official; the peons are his servants.

course not considering politicals. Most of them are so much steeped in error that they may be considered past reform.) If this objective is once accepted, it would result in a complete overhauling of the prison system. At present few prison officials have even heard of such a notion. I have a recollection that the old United Province Jail Manual had a paragraph pointing out that the prisoner's work was not meant to be productive or useful; its object was punitive. This was almost an ideal statement of what a prison should not be. That paragraph has since gone but the spirit still remains—a spirit that is harsh and punitive and utterly lacking in humanity. The list of prison offences in the United Provinces Jail Manual is an amazing one. It contains all that the wit of man can devise to make life as intolerable as possible. Talking, singing, loud laughing, visiting latrines at other than stated hours, not eating the food given, etc., etc., are among the offences. It is not surprising that all the energy of the gaol staff goes in suppressing the prisoner and preventing him from doing the hundred and one things forbidden him.

Ignorant people imagine that if the punishment is not severe enough crimes will increase. As a matter of fact, the exact reverse is the truth. A century ago in England, petty thieves were hung. When it was proposed to abolish the death penalty for thieves, there was a tremendous outcry and noble lords stated in the House of Lords that this would result in thieves and robbers seizing everything and creating a reign of terror. As a matter of fact the reform had the opposite effect and crime went down. Crime has steadily gone down in England and other countries as the criminal law and prisons have been bettered. Many old prisons in England are not required as prisons now and are used for other purposes. In India, it is well known that the prison population goes on increasing (quite apart from political prisoners) and the executive and judiciary help in this process by encouraging long and barbarous sentences. The imprisonment of the young is universally considered to be a most demoralizing system and is avoided. Here in India gaols are full of young men and boys and frequently they are sentenced to whipping.

Another error which people indulge in is the fear that if gaol conditions are improved people will flock in! This shows a singular ignorance of human nature. No one wants to go to prison however good the prison might be. To be deprived of liberty and family life and friends and home surroundings is a terrible thing. It is well known that the Indian peasant will prefer to stick to his ancestral soil and starve rather than go elsewhere to better his condition. To improve prison conditions does not mean that prison life should be made soft; it means that it should be made human and sensible. There should be hard work, but not the barbarous and wasteful labour of the oil pumps or water pumps or mills. The prison should produce goods either in large-scale modern factories where prisoners work, or in cottage industries. All work should be useful from the point of view of the prison as well as the future of the prisoner, and the work should be paid for at market rates, minus the cost of maintenance of the prisoner. After a hard eight-hour day's work the prisoners should be encouraged to co-operate together in various activities—games, sports, reading, recitals, lectures. They should above all be encouraged to laugh and develop human contacts with the prison staff and other prisoners. Every prisoner's education must be attended to, not only in just the three R's, but something more, wherever possible. The mind of the prisoner should be cultivated and the prison library, to which there must be free access, should have plenty of good books. Reading and writing should be encouraged in every way and that means that every prisoner should be allowed to have writing materials and books. Nothing is more harmful to the prisoner than to spend twelve to fourteen hours at a stretch every evening locked up in the cell or barrack with absolutely nothing to do. A Sunday or holiday means for him a much longer period of locking up.

Selected newspapers are essential to keep the prisoner in touch with the world, and interviews and letters should be made as frequent and informal as possible. Personally, I think that weekly interviews and letters should be permitted. The prisoner should be made to feel as far as possible that he or she is a human being and brutal and degrading punishments must be avoided.'

All this sounds fantastic when compared with present-day prison conditions in India. And yet I have only suggested what the prisons of most of the advanced countries already have. Indeed they have much more. Our present administration, and indeed our Government itself, cannot understand or appreciate this as they have successfully imprisoned their own minds in prisons of dull routine. But public opinion must begin to demand these changes so that, when the time comes, they might be introduced without difficulty.

It must not be thought that these changes will involve much extra expenditure. If properly run on modern industrial lines the prisons can not only be self-supporting but can actually make a profit after providing for all the additional amenities suggested. There is absolutely no difficulty in introducing the changes except one—the absolute necessity of having a competent, human staff fully understanding and appreciating the new angle of vision and eager to work it.

I wish some of our people would study and, where possible, personally inspect, prison conditions in foreign countries. They will find how our prisons lag far behind them. The new human element is imposing itself everywhere, as also a recognition of the fact that a criminal is largely created by social conditions and, instead of being punished, has to be treated as for a disease. Real criminals are infantile in mind and it is folly to treat them as grown-ups. A delightful book which stressed this point humorously long ago is Samuel Butler's *Erewhon*.

In the prisons of the little country of Latvia even, we are told that "everything is done to create a homely atmosphere in the rooms and cells with plants, flowers, books and such personal belongings of the prisoners as photographs, handicrafts, and wireless sets." Prisoners are paid for their work, half the earnings accumulating and the other half being spent by prisoners on extra food, tobacco, newspapers, etc.

Russia, that terrible land of the Soviets, has perhaps gone farthest ahead in the improvement of prison conditions. Recently a competent observer inspected the Soviet prisons and his report is interesting. This observer was an eminent English lawyer, D. N. Pritt, K.C., who is also the Chairman of the Howard League for Penal Reform—an organization which has been the pioneer of prison reform in England for more than sixty years. Pritt tells us that the punitive character of punishment has been entirely removed and it is considered purely reformatory now. The treatment of prisoners is humane and remarkably good.

There are two types of prisons: (1) Semi-open camps or fully open communes or colonies. These are really not prisons at all; prisoners live a village life subject to certain restrictions. (2) Closed prisons. These are the hardest type of prisons and yet even here there is a surprising amount of freedom for the prisoners. There is a feeling of equality between warders and prisoners and unrestricted intercourse, except in working hours, with other prisoners or with guards. There is normal factory work for eight hours a day at normal wages. For the rest there are games, education, gymnastics, lectures, wireless, books, and amateur dramatic performances by the prisoners. The prisoners also produce a wall newspaper and do not hesitate to criticize warders and other prison officials in it "for having forgotten that a prison is not for punishment, but for reformation."

The principle of self-government, which is encouraged in all institutions in Russia, is even practised to some extent in the prisons, the prisoners imposing penalties on themselves. Smoking is allowed except when at work. Frequent interviews are permitted and a virtually unrestricted and uncensored writing and reception of letters. And, most remarkable rule of all, almost always the prisoner is allowed a fortnight's summer holiday to go home to look after the harvest, etc. In the case of a woman prisoner who has a baby, she can either keep the baby in the prison crèche, where the baby will be properly looked after, or leave the baby at home. In the latter event the mother is allowed to go home several times a day to feed it!

There were flowers, pictures, and photographs in the cells. Prisoners were regularly examined by psychiatrists to find out if their mental condition was satisfactory. Whenever necessary, prisoners were removed to mental hospitals for treatment. Solitary confinement was very rare.

Hardly credible! And yet there it is and the results of this humane treatment have been surprisingly good. The Russians hope to reduce crime substantially and to shut up most of their prisons. So the good treatment does not eventually fill up the gaols but empties them, provided the economic background is suitable and work is to be had.

A short while ago there was a meeting in the House of Commons to consider the protection of animals in India. A very laudable object. But it is worth remembering that the two-legged animal, *homo sapiens*, in

India is also worthy of care and protection—especially those who undergo the long physical and mental torture of prison life and come out with an impaired capacity for normal life.

Every prison cell in Norway has an inscription on its walls. It is a quotation from a speech of a famous Norwegian prisoner, Lars Olsen Skrefsund, who served a long sentence for theft when drunk, came out to India afterwards and founded the Scandinavian Santal* Mission. He became a great linguist knowing seventeen languages, ancient and modern, and among them of course was the Santal language. The passage in his speech which is exhibited in the prison cells runs as follows:

"Nobody can imagine what a prisoner feels but one who has at some time felt what it is to be a prisoner. Some idea of it may be formed, but this cannot express the feelings of the man who sits sad and forsaken in his cell."

It is well that those whom fate or fortune keep out of the prison cell give thought sometimes to that sad and forsaken figure.

* The Santals are a pre-Aryan people who live in Bengal and adjoining districts.

5

THE MIND OF A JUDGE*

THE days when I practised at the Bar as a lawyer seem distant and far-off, and I find it a little difficult now to recapture the thoughts and moods that must have possessed me then. And yet it was only sixteen years ago that I walked out of the web of the law in more ways than one. Sometimes I look back on those days, for in prison one grows retrospective and, as the present is dull and monotonous and full of unhappiness, the past stands out, vivid and inviting. There was little that was inviting in that legal past of mine, and at no time have I felt the urge to revert to it. But still my mind played with the ifs and possibilities of that past—a foolish but an entertaining pastime when inaction is thrust on one—and I wondered how life would have treated me if I had stuck to my original profession. That was not an unlikely contingency, though it seems odd enough now; a slight twist in the thread of life might have changed my whole future. I suppose I would have done tolerably well at the Bar, and I would have had a much more peaceful, a duller, and physically a more comfortable existence than I have so far had. Perhaps I might even have developed into a highly respectable and solemn-looking judge with wig and gown, as quite

* Written in prison, September 1935. First published in the *Modern Review*, Calcutta.

a number of my old friends and colleagues have done.

How would I have felt as a judge, I have wondered? How does a judge feel or think? This second question used to occupy my mind to some extent even when I was in practice conducting or watching criminal cases, lost in wonder at the speed and apparent unconcern with which the judge sent men to the scafford or long terms of imprisonment. That question, in a more personal form, has always faced me when I have stood in the prisoner's dock and awaited sentence, or attended a friend's trial for political offences. That question is almost always with me in prison, surrounded as I am with hundreds or thousands of persons whom judges have sent there. (I am not concerned for the moment with political offenders; I am only referring to the ordinary prisoners.) The judge had considered the evil deed that was done, and he had meted out justice and punishment as he had been told to do by the penal code. Sometimes he had added a sermon of his own, probably to justify a particularly heavy sentence. He had not given a thought to the upbringing, environment, education (or want of it) of the prisoner before him. He had paid no heed to the psychological background that led to the deed, or to the mental conflict that had raged within that dumb, frightened creature who stands in the dock. He had no notion that perhaps society, of which he considers himself a pillar and an ornament, might be partly responsible for the crime that he is judging.

He is, let us presume, a conscientious judge, and he weighs the evidence carefully before pronouncing sentence. He may even give the benefit of the doubt to the accused, though our judges are not given to doubting very much. But, almost invariably, the prisoner and he belong to different worlds with very little in common between them, and incapable of understanding each other. There may sometimes be an intellectual appreciation of the other's outlook and background, though that is rare enough, but there is no emotional awareness of it, and without the latter there can never be true understanding of another person.

Sentence follows, and these sentences are remarkable. As the realization comes that crime is not decreasing, and may even be increasing, the sentences become more savage in the hope that this may frighten the evil-doer. The judge and the power behind the judge have not grasped the fact that crime may be due to special reasons, which might be investigated, and that some of these may be capable of control; and, further, that in any event a harsh penal code does not improve the social morals of a group, or a harsh sentence those of an individual who has lapsed from grace. The only remedy they know, both for political and non-political offences, is punishment and an attempt to terrorize the offender by what are called deterrent sentences. The usual political sentence now for a speech or a song or a poem which offends the Government is two years' rigorous imprisonment (in the Frontier Province it is three years), and a lavish use of this is being made from day to day; but even this seems trivial when compared with the cases of large numbers of those people who are kept confined for four or five years or more, indefinitely, without conviction or sentence.

Political cases, however, depend greatly on the moods of Government and a changing situation, and do not help us in considering the ordinary administration of the criminal law. To some extent the two overlap and affect each other; for instance, many agrarian and labour cases in courts are often definitely political in origin. It is also well known that many people, who are considered politically undesirable by the police, are proceeded against under the bad livelihood or similar section of the Code and clapped in prison as bad characters with no special offence being brought up against them. Ignoring such cases and considering what might be called the unadulterated crimes, two facts stand out: both the numbers of convictions and the length of sentences are growing. Every year the various provincial prison reports complain of the increasing number of prisoners and the necessity of additional accommodation. The peak years, when the civil disobedience movement sent its scores of thousands to prison, become the normal years even without this special influx of politicals. Occasionally the difficulty is overcome by discharging a few thousand short-timers before their time, but the strain continues.

The Central Prisons are full of "lifers," prisoners sentenced for life, and others sentenced to long terms.

Most of these "lifers" come in huge bunches in dacoity cases, and probably a fair proportion are guilty, though I am inclined to think that many innocent persons are involved also, as the evidence is entirely one of identification. It is obvious that the growing number of dacoities is due to the increasing unemployment and poverty of the masses as well as the lower middle classes. Most of the other criminal offences involving property are also due to this terrible prospect of want and starvation that faces the vast majority of our people.

Do our judges ever realize this, or give thought to the despair that the sight of a starving wife or children might produce even in a normal human being? Is a man to sit helplessly by and see his dear ones sicken and die for want of the simplest human necessities? He slips and offends against the law, and the law and the judge then see to it that he can never again become a normal person with a socially beneficial job of work. They help to produce the criminal type, so-called, and then are surprised to find that such types exist and multiply.

The major offences lead to a life sentence, or ten years or so. But the petty offences and the way they are treated by judges are even more instructive. The vast majority of these are buried in court files and get no publicity; only rarely do the papers mention such a case. Three such cases, taken almost at random from recent issues of newspapers, are given below:

Rahman was an old offender with twelve previous convictions, the first of which dated back to 1913.

The present offence was one of theft of clothes valued at a few rupees. Rahman pleaded guilty, and requested the court to send him to a reformatory or some such place from where he could emerge thoroughly reformed. The judge, who was the Judicial Commissioner in Sind, refused this request, and sentenced him to seven years, adding: "If this seven-year sentence of hard labour does not reform you, God alone must come to your aid." (Karachi: May 23, 1935.)

Badri, who had four previous convictions, was sentenced to two years' rigorous imprisonment under Sections 411/75 Indian Penal Code for having dishonestly received a stolen *chadder* (cloth sheet). (Lucknow: July 3, 1935.)

Ghulam Mohammad, an old offender, was sentenced to three years' rigorous imprisonment for stealing one rupee by picking the pocket of a man. (Sialkot: July 15, 1935.)

These and similar sentences may be perfectly correct from the point of view of the Indian Penal Code, but it does seem to me astonishing that any judge should imagine that by inflicting such sentences he is reforming the offender. Evidently the Judicial Commissioner in Sind had himself some doubts about the efficacy of his treatment, for he hinted that God might be given a chance on the next occasion.

There they sit, these judges, in their courts, and a procession of unfortunates passes before them—some go to the scaffold, some to be whipped, some to imprisonment, to which may be added solitary confinement. They are doing their duty according to their abstract ideas of justice and punishment; they must consider themselves as the protectors of society from anti-social criminal elements. Do their thoughts ever go beyond these set ideas and take human shape, considering the miserable offender as a human being with parents, wife, children, friends? They punish the individual, but at the same time they punish a group also, for the ripples of suffering spread out and go far. Those who have to die at least die swiftly, the agony is brief. But the agony is long for those who enter prison.

> Behind the door, within the wall
> Locked, they sit the numbered ones. . . .

Two years, three years, seven years stolen from life's brief span—each year of twelve months, each month of thirty days, each day of twenty-four hours—how terribly long it all seems to the prisoner, how wearily time passes!

All this is very sad and deplorable, no doubt, but what is the poor judge to do? Is he to wallow in a sea of sentimentality and give up sentencing offenders against the laws? If he is so soft and sensitive he is not much good as a judge, and will have to give place to another. No, no one expects the judge to embrace every offender and invite him to dinner, but a human element in a trial and sentence would certainly improve matters. The judges are too impersonal, distant, and too little aware of the consequences of the sentences they award. If their awareness could be increased, as well as a sense of fellow-feeling with the prisoner, it would be a great gain. This can only come when the two belong to more or less the same class. A financier who has embezzled vast sums of public money will have every sympathy from the judge, not so the poor wretch who has picked up a rupee or stolen a sheet to satisfy an urgent need. For the judge and the average offender to belong to the same class means a fundamental change in the social structure, as indeed every great reform does. But even apart from, and in anticipation of, that, something could certainly be done.

It was Bernard Shaw, I think, who suggested that every judge and magistrate, as well as every prison official, should spend a period in prison, living like ordinary prisoners. Only then would they be justified in sentencing people to imprisonment, or to governing them there. The suggestion is an excellent one, although it may be difficult to give effect to it. I ventured to suggest it once to the Home Member and the Inspector-General of Prisons of the United Provinces Government for their personal adoption, but they did not seem to favour it. At least one well-known prison official, however, has adopted it. This was Thomas Mott Osborne, of the famous Sing Sing prison in New York. He trained himself by undergoing a term of voluntary imprisonment, and, as a result of this, he introduced later on many remarkable improvements in the social rehabilitation and education of the prisoners.

Such a term of voluntary imprisonment will do a world of good to the bodies and souls of our judges, magistrates, and prison officials. It will also give them a greater insight into prison life. But obviously no such voluntary effort can ever approach the real thing. The sting of imprisonment will be absent as well as the peculiarly helpless and broken feeling before the armed and walled power of the State, which a prisoner experiences. Nor will the voluntary prisoner ever have to face bad treatment from the staff. The essence of prison is a psychological background of having been cast off from society like a diseased limb. That will necessarily be absent. But with all these drawbacks the experience will be worth while, and will help in making the administration of the criminal law more human and beneficial. The great invasions of our prisons by middle-class people during the non-co-operation and civil disobedience movements had indirectly a marked effect. As the prison-goers did not become judges or prison officials the direct effect was little. But a knowledge of prison conditions and a sympathy for the prisoner's lot became widespread, and public opinion and the crusading efforts of some Congressmen bore substantial results.

I do not know whether I am over-soft, but I do not think I err on the mushy and sentimental side. Other people, and even many of my close colleagues, have considered me rather hard. Mr. C. R. Das once referred to me at a meeting of the All-India Congress Committee as being "cold-blooded." Perhaps it all depends on the standard of comparison as well as on the fact that some display their emotions more than others. However that may be, I do hate the idea of punishment, and especially "deterrent" punishment and all the suffering, deliberately caused, that it involves. Perhaps it cannot be done away with completely in this present-day world of ours, but it can certainly be minimized, toned down, and almost humanized.

At one time I was strongly opposed to the death penalty, and, in theory, my opposition still continues. But I have come to realize that there are many things far worse than death, and if the choice had to be made, and I was given it, I would probably accept a death sentence rather than one of imprisonment for life. But I would not like to be hung; I would prefer being shot or guillotined, or even electrocuted; most of all other methods I would like to be given, as Socrates was of old, the cup of poison which would send me to sleep from which there was no awaking. This last method seems to me to be far the most civilized and humane. But in India we favour hangings, and last year the official mind showed us the texture of which it was made by organizing public hangings in Karachi, or somewhere else in Sind. This was meant to terrify would-be evil-doers. It turned out to be a huge *mela*, where thousands gathered to witness the ghastly spectacle. I suppose the mentality behind such public exhibitions bears a family resemblance to that which prompted the *autos da fé* of the Spanish Inquisition.

A friend of mine who became a High Court Judge had a "crisis of conscience" when he had first to sentence a man to death. The idea seemed hateful to him. He overcame his repugnance, however (he had to, or else he would not have long continued in his job), and I suppose he soon got used to sending people to the scaffold without turning a hair. He was an exception, and I doubt if many others in his position have ever had such scruples. It is probably easier to sentence a man to death than to see the sentence carried out. And yet even sensitive people get used to this painful sight. A young English member of the Indian Civil Service had to attend hangings in the local gaol. At his first hanging, he told me, he was thoroughly sick and felt bad all day. But very soon the sight had no unusual effect on him whatever, and he used to go straight from the execution to his breakfast-table and have a hearty meal.

I have never seen a death sentence being carried out. In most of the gaols where I have lived as a prisoner executions did not take place, but on three or four occasions there were hangings in my gaol. These took place in a special enclosure, cut off from the rest of the prison, but the whole gaol population knew of it, perhaps because the unlocking of the various barracks and cells took place at a later hour on those mornings. I experienced a peculiar feeling on those days, an ominous stillness, and a tendency for people to talk in low voices. It is possible that all this was the product of my own imagination.

And yet with all my repugnance for executions, I feel that some method of eliminating utterly undesirable human beings will have to be adopted and used with discretion. The real objection to the infliction of capital punishment as well as other punishments is of course not so much the resultant suffering of the person punished, as the brutalization of the community that authorizes such punishment, and more particularly of the individuals who carry it out. This is especially noticeable in the case of whipping, which is widely prevalent in India. The official defence for the punishment of whipping is that it is meant for horrible crimes, like rape with violence. In practice it has a much wider range, and in 1932 (as was stated in the British House of Commons) five hundred civil disobedience prisoners were whipped. This was the official figure, unofficial gaol beatings not being included. These political prisoners were whipped either for purely political offences or for breaches of gaol discipline. No violence or crime was involved. It has now been laid down officially that in serious cases of hunger-strike in gaol whipping may be resorted to. We thus have it that in the opinion of the British Government in India a hunger-strike or breaches of gaol discipline stand on the same level as rape with violence.

Whipping is usually administered in prisons by some low caste prisoner. No prisoner likes the job, but he has little choice in the matter. The higher caste prisoners would in any event refuse to whip, and even the warders are reluctant to do so. A case came to my notice once when a warder was asked to whip. He refused absolutely, and was punished for this contumacy. It is interesting to compare the sensitiveness to whipping of the prisoners and warders with that of our judges and prison officials who order it, and our Government which authorizes and defends it.

I was reading the other day about the film censorship in Britain. It was stated that one of the grounds for censorship was the avoidance of cruelty scenes. In animal films no kill was to be shown. Films "showing pain or suffering on the part of an animal, whether such pain is caused by accident or intention" are not allowed as these are supposed to have a bad effect on spectators, especially children, and "undermine moral character."

We also in India have our film censorships and an active Society for the Prevention of Cruelty to Animals. Unfortunately human beings are not included in the category of animals, and so they cannot benefit by the activities of the Society. And our film censorship justifies itself by banning films dealing with "Quetta Earthquake Topical," or "National Congress Scenes," or "Departure of Mahatma Gandhi for the Round Table Conference," and similar dangerous topics.

Sentences of death and whipping impress us and pain us, but, after all, they affect only a very small number of the scores of thousands who are sentenced by our courts. The vast majority of these go to prison, mostly for long periods over which their punishment is spread out. It is a continuing torture, a never-ceasing pain, till mind itself grows dull and the body is blunted to sensation. The criminal type develops, the ugly fruit of our gaols and our criminal law, and there is no fitting him in then with the social machine outside. He is the square peg everywhere, with no roots, no home, suspicious of everybody, being suspected everywhere, till at last he comes back to his only true resting-place, the prison, and takes up again the tin or iron bowl which is his faithful companion there. Do our judges ever trouble to think of cause and effect, of the inevitable consequences of an act or decision? Do they realize that their courts and the prisons are the principal factories for the production and stamping of the criminal type?

In prison one comes to realize more than anywhere else the basic nature of the State; it is the force, the compulsion, the violence of the governing group. "Government," George Washington is reported to have said, "is not reason, it is not eloquence—it is force! Like fire, it is a dangerous servant and a fearful master." It is true that civilization has been built up on co-operation and forbearance and mutual collaboration in a thousand ways. But when a crisis comes and the State is afraid of some danger then the superstructure goes, or, at any rate, is subordinated to the primary function of the State—self-protection by force and violence. The army, the police, the prison come into greater prominence then, and of the three the prison is perhaps the nakedest form of a State in miniature.

Must the State always be based on force and violence, or will the day come when this element of compulsion is reduced to a minimum and almost fades away? That day, if it ever comes, is still far off. Meanwhile the violence of the governing group produces the violence of other groups that seek to oust it. It is a vicious circle, violence breeding violence, and on ethical grounds there is little to choose between the two violences. It always seems curious to me how the governing group in a State, basing itself on an extremity of violence, objects on moral or ethical grounds to the force or violence of others. On practical grounds of self-protection they have reason to object, but why drag in morality and ethics? State violence is preferable to private violence in many ways, for one major violence is far better than numerous petty private violences. State violence is also likely to be a more or less ordered violence, and thus preferable to the disorderly violence of private groups and individuals, for even in violence order is better than disorder, except that this makes the State more efficient in its violence and powers of compulsion. But when a State goes off the rails completely and begins to indulge in disorderly violence, then indeed it is a terrible thing, and no private or individual effort can compete with it in horror and brutality.

"You must live in a chaos if you would give birth to a dancing star," says Nietzsche. Must it be so? Is there no other way? The old difficulty of the humanist is ever cropping up, his disgust at force and violence and cruelty, and yet his inability to overcome these by merely standing by and looking on. That is the recurring theme of Ernst Toller's plays:

> The sword, as ever, is a shift of fools
> To hide their folly.
>
> By force, the smoky torch of violence,
> We shall not find the way.

Yet force and violence reign triumphant to-day everywhere. Only in our country has a noble effort been made to combat them by means other than those of force. The inspiration of that effort, and of the leader who lifted us out of our petty selves by his matchless purity of outlook, still remains, though the ultimate outcome be shrouded in darkness.

But these are big questions beyond the power even of judges. We may not perhaps be able to find an answer to them in our time; or, finding an answer, be unable to impress it on wayward humanity. Meanwhile, the smaller questions and problems pursue us and we cannot ignore them. We come back to the job of the judge and the prison governor, and we can say this, at least, with certainty: that the deliberate infliction of punishment or torture of the mind or body is not the way to reform anyone, that though this may break or twist the victim it will not mend him, that it is much more likely to brutalize and deform him who inflicts it. For the inevitable effect of cruelty and torture is to degrade both the sufferer and the person who causes the suffering.

6

QUETTA*

IT is curious how sometimes a relatively minor event impresses one more than a major happening. Trivial words or gestures are apt to reveal an individual far more than his studied poses and utterances. So also with nations and peoples and governments. I suppose most people will agree that one of the outstanding events of recent times in India was the shooting down of large numbers of unarmed men and women by General Dyer and his soldiery in the Jallianwala Bagh,† and the consequences of this deed were far-reaching. Amritsar, indeed, has become something more than a city of the Punjab, or even the holy place of Sikhism. It typifies the world over a particularly brutal method of dealing with subject peoples. And yet, ghastly as all this was, I have never had much difficulty in understanding the mentality of a Dyer, and because of that feeling of at least partial understanding, my resentment against him personally has probably been far less than that of most other Indians. It is true that he made his case unpardonable and wholly inexcusable by his arrogance and vulgar bragging before the Hunter Committee of Inquiry. But even that had a psychological explanation and,

* Written in prison, August 1935. Not previously published.
† In 1919.

granting the vulgarity and the jingoism, the rest more or less followed.

What affected me far more, and I imagine there were many others who felt this way, was the reaction in England to Dyer's deed and his evidence. Officially he was mildly reprimanded, and there were no doubt many individuals who condemned him and some newspapers that criticized him strongly. But the real reaction of the British ruling classes was never in doubt. It was clear as daylight, and the *Morning Post* and the House of Lords and the subscription raised for General Dyer shouted it out to the world. This cold-blooded approval of that deed shocked me greatly. It seemed absolutely immoral, indecent; to use public school language, it was the height of bad form. I realized then, more vividly than I had ever done before, how brutal and immoral imperialism was and how it had eaten into the souls of the British upper classes.

My mind went back to this revealing instance the other day when I read about the refusal of the Government of India to allow Gandhiji and Rajendra Prasad, the President of the Congress for the year, to visit Quetta after the great earthquake. That refusal, a trivial enough affair, was yet most revealing of the mentality of Government. Inevitably, one thought of the contrast when last year, in connection with another great earthquake, Gandhiji had offered, on behalf of the Committee, of which Rajendra Babu was the honoured head, whole-hearted and "respectful" co-operation to the Government. That co-operation was worth having, as Rajendra Prasad's Committee had almost as big a fund at its disposal as the Government, with all its resources in India and England, had managed to collect; even more, it was valuable because of the fine village organization of workers behind Rajendra Babu and his colleagues. It is also worth remembering that this co-operation was offered even though in theory civil disobedience of a kind continued and many prominent Congressmen were in prison.

That contrast was marked. But even apart from that the obvious course for any sensible Government would have been to invite the co-operation of Rajendra Prasad after the fine work he did in the Behar earthquake and the great experience he gained thereby. There must be very few persons in India to-day who can rival him in knowledge of earthquake relief work. In all probability he knows far more of the subject than all the members of the Governor-General's Executive Council and their various secretaries taken together.

Another equally obvious thing to do, in order to gain public support and co-operation, was to take a number of public men and newspaper men into the Government's confidence, give them full facilities to visit the earthquake area, and discuss the situation frankly with them. This would not have tied the hands of Government in any way, and it is absurd to say that some additional arrivals in the affected area would have upset the food situation or the sanitary measures that were being taken. Such newcomers would have made their own food arrangements, and if they risked catching an infectious disease that was their look out. It was not a question of crowds of outsiders rolling in and interfering with all arrangements.

But our benign Government has an astonishing knack of doing the wrong thing, and even on the rare occasions when it does the right thing it does it in a wrong way. And then it is painfully surprised when it finds that the purity of its motives is suspected and cheering crowds do not welcome its efforts with enthusiasm.

There was no room for Gandhiji or Rajendra Babu or other popular leaders and well-known relief workers in Quetta, but Boy Scouts could be sent without danger of their catching disease or lessening the stock of food. If Gandhiji had gone there might have been a shortage of goat's milk and dates.

Quetta became one of the battle-fronts, enveloped as it were in the fog of war, a no-man's land which was cut off from the rest of the country. The official megaphone boomed out its version of the news to us and told us of the wonders that were being performed by the official agency alone and unaided by others.

> I am the blessed Glendoveer,
> 'Tis mine to speak and yours to hear.

True there were also the Simla correspondents of certain favoured newspapers, those wise and clever mortals who are not like unto other men, and who can even glimpse, as through a glass darkly, the mysterious workings of the godlike mind of the Government of India.

It was not unnatural or unexpected that these arrangements should meet with the disapproval of less favoured newspaper men and others. Nor was it at all surprising that they should, under the circumstances, give credence and publicity to vague rumours, many of them exaggerated or even unfounded. That was very wrong, of course, but human nature is weak, and it is not possible for all of us to live up to the high and noble standards set in Simla or New Delhi. Exclude a newspaper man and you make him suspicious and capable of believing almost anything. Two or three years ago the Soviet Government prevented all newspaper men from going to the Caucasus. The journalists scented trouble, something that the Soviet wanted to hide. It was a huge famine said some; others inclined to the view that a nationalist rebellion had broken out in Georgia and parts of the Ukraine. The argument is still going on, and it is by no means clear what took place then in those forbidden regions. Most people very rightly imagine that something not creditable to the Soviet Government must have occurred, else why this hush-hush policy? And the Soviet can hardly complain if rumours and exaggerated accounts are believed.

So also a number of Indian newspapers, excited and displeased at the official attitude about Quetta, gave publicity to such scraps of news as rumour brought them. And then the Press Act and various emergency measures descended heavily on these hapless papers with their forfeits and securities. A large sum of money went from the newspapers to the provincial governments. The majesty of the Government had been vindicated. Truth had prevailed, as it was bound to, in the end, and the serpent of falsehood had been crushed by the swift action of various magistrates and governors and the like.

I have absolutely no idea what these items of news or comments were to which Government objected. It really does not much matter what they were, and I am prepared to assume that they were thoroughly objectionable. What seems to me much more important is the extraordinary attitude of the Government throughout this Quetta business. They took one false step after another—perhaps each subsequent step was made inevitable by the previous one—and made a horrid mess of a simple business. Who could have thought that even an earthquake could be bungled in this manner? And it is this bungling that reveals as in a flash that curious compound of conceit, ideas of prestige, intolerance, a certain cleverness, distrust, fear, and stupidity which go to make up the mind of the Government of India.

I do not mean that the actual relief work in Quetta was bungled. I have no knowledge of that, but I am inclined to think that official agency, even when efficient, lacks the human touch and is often wasteful. I imagine that the addition of non-officials to the workers, especially in the villages round about Quetta city, would have gone a long way to supply this human touch. Personally I am not a believer even in the efficiency of official processes. But as the relief work was in charge of the military it was probably far more efficient than the civil side of Government would have been.

It was indeed fortunate for Quetta that a large force of military was stationed there, and they could immediately start relief operations. Disciplined soldiers are the best workers in such an emergency, especially in the early days. In any event the British and Indian soldiery would have worked hard and earnestly at the task; the fact that their own comrades had perished in the catastrophe must have added to their zeal. Unfortunately, but very naturally, the army is not popular with the people. It is looked upon as something foreign, meant and used from time to time to keep them down. The Indian soldiers are definitely mercenary, the British troops foreigners wholly ignorant of the land they are serving in, and both of them are looked upon with fear and dislike by the people. Especially is the Tommy the object of this distrust. There are no points of contact between him and the people, and there are numerous barriers separating them. Even our B.A.s and M.A.s, on the rare occasions when they meet Tommies, find it difficult to get over the language difficulty. Their training in Shakespeare and Milton has not qualified them to understand the cockney speech, or the broad Lancashire and Yorkshire dialect, or English as she is spoken across the Tweed.

This gulf and the fear and distrust of the military are unfortunate. The Indian soldier is very much the peasant we know with a thin veneer of soldiering over him; the British Tommy is a very simple and likeable creature, rather shy, and afraid of himself in strange surroundings, but always willing to expand and grow friendly if approached in the right way. The two, with the discipline and organization behind them, were ideal workers in the earthquake area, and it was well that they were utilized immediately. But however good they might have been, they could not supply all the human needs of the people, nor could they easily get rid of the distrust which had long been associated with them.

It seems to me that it was also very proper on the part of Government to regulate the entry of people into the earthquake area. Large numbers of odd people, bent on doing relief work after their own fashion, might easily have created confusion and hindered work rather than helped it. But to regulate entry is one thing, to close and seal the area as if it was a theatre of war is quite another. I do not know if any military considerations prompted this secretive policy, for the frontier is not far from Quetta. But no considerations could possibly justify the deliberate and offensive exclusion of noted public men who were offering their services in a spirit of co-operation. It is quite inconceivable that any such attitude could have been taken up in any other country that is supposed to be civilized. Only a Government arrogantly irresponsive to popular feeling could have acted in this way.

Why did the Government of India act in this manner, I wondered, for whatever its actions might be, it has to bow down to some extent to the spirit of the times, and to talk of co-operation and the like. The only answer I could find was that the Government had Gandhi and the Congress on the brain. It is not for me to object to this obsession of theirs; I think they have some justification for it. But it seems to lead them into curious corners. A psychologist would probably give a satisfactory explanation of this by reference to some complex. Gandhi and the Congress are both nuisances; therefore let us ignore them, sit on them. If our superiority is not sufficiently recognized, let us proclaim it ourselves and compel people to listen to us; let us collect chits emphasizing this superiority and praising our good works. If we are not tall enough, let us stand on tip-toe; people will surely be impressed.

Perhaps it is some such unconscious functioning of the mind that forms the background of much that Government does. The old desire to keep up prestige means in the end some kind of attempt to stand on one's toes, in the vain hope of adding to one's size. But this is hardly a dignified procedure, and seldom deceives. Often it has the opposite effect.

So it was in this Quetta business. The attempt of Government to snub Gandhi and the Congress resulted in the Government being shown up for what it was, through its hurried attempts to justify itself, and its unseemly anger at its critics. The Congress and Gandhi did rather well. There was dignity in their attitude; there was no shouting, no outward anger, no official remonstrance even.

Our high officers of Government move about with

pomp and circumstance, their surroundings impress us, their gilded liveries of office dazzle us, they address us from time to time in stately, if somewhat trite, phrases pointing out the error of our ways. They cultivate the calm and dignified demeanour of the great.

> They think that dignity of soul may come,
> Perchance, with dignity of body.

Perhaps it helps a little. But even dignity of body is not very evident when one is standing on one's toes.

7

FIRST LETTER TO INDIRA*

FOR INDIRA PRIYADARSHINI ON HER THIRTEENTH BIRTHDAY

ON your birthday you have been in the habit of receiving presents and good wishes. Good wishes you will still have in full measure, but what present can I give you from Naini Prison? My presents cannot be very material or solid. They can only be of the air and of the mind and spirit, such as a good fairy might have bestowed on you—something that even the high walls of prison cannot stop.

You know, sweetheart, how I dislike sermonizing and doling out good advice. When I am tempted to do this I always think of a story of a "very wise man" I once read. Perhaps one day you will yourself read the book which contains this story. Thirteen hundred years ago there came a great traveller from China to India in search of wisdom and knowledge. His name was Hiuen Tsang and over the deserts and mountains of the north he came, braving many dangers, facing and overcoming many obstacles, so great was his thirst

* Written in prison, October 26, 1930, and published in *Glimpses of World History*, Allahabad, 1934. Indira's birthday takes place, according to the Gregorian Calendar, on November 19th. It was observed, however, on October 26th according to the *Samvat* era.

for knowledge. And he spent many years in India learning himself and teaching others, especially at the great university of Nalanda, which existed then near the city that was called Pātaliputra and is now known as Patna. Hiuen Tsang became very learned himself and he was given the title of "Master of the Law"—the Law of the Buddha—and he journeyed all over India and saw and studied the people that lived in this great country in those far-off days. Later he wrote a book of his travels, and it is this book which contains the story that comes to my mind. It is about a man from South India who came to Karnasuvarna, which was a city somewhere near modern Bhagalpur in Behar; and this man, it is written, wore round his belly and waist copper-plates, and on his head he carried a lighted torch. Staff in hand, with proud bearing and lofty steps, he wandered about in this strange attire. And when anyone asked him the reason for this curious get-up, he told him that his wisdom was so great that he was afraid his belly would burst if he did not wear copper-plates round it; and because he was moved with pity for the ignorant people round about him, who lived in darkness, he carried the light on his head.

Well, I am quite sure that there is no danger of my ever bursting with too much wisdom and so there is no need for me to wear copper-plates or armour. And in any event, I hope that my wisdom, such of it as I possess, does not live in my belly. Wherever it may reside, there is plenty of room still for more of it and there is no chance of there being no room left. If I am so limited in wisdom how can I pose as a wise man to others and distribute good advice to all? And so I have always thought that the best way to find out what is right and what is not right, what should be done and what should not be done, is not to give a sermon, but to talk and discuss, and out of the discussion sometimes a little bit of the truth comes out. I have liked my talks with you and we have discussed many things, but the world is wide and beyond our world lie other wonderful and mysterious worlds, so none of us need ever be bored or imagine, like the very foolish and conceited person whose story Hiuen Tsang has told us, that we have learned everything worth learning and become very wise. And perhaps it is as well that we do not become very wise; for the very wise, if any such there are, must sometimes feel rather sad that there is nothing more to learn. They must miss the joy of discovery and of learning new things—the great adventure that all of us who care may have.

I must not therefore sermonize. But what am I to do then? A letter can hardly take the place of a talk; at best it is a one-sided affair. So, if I say anything that sounds like good advice do not take it as if it was a bad pill to swallow. Imagine that I have made a suggestion to you for you to think over, as if we really were having a talk.

In your history books you read of great periods in the life of nations. We read of great men and women and great deeds performed, and sometimes in our dreams and reveries we imagine ourselves back in those times and doing brave deeds like the heroes and heroines of old. Do you remember how fascinated you were when you first read the story of Jeanne d'Arc, and how your ambition was to do something like her? Ordinary men and women are not usually heroic. They think of their daily bread and butter, of their children, of their household worries and the like. But a time comes when a whole people become full of faith for a great cause, and then even simple, ordinary men and women become heroes, and history becomes stirring and epoch-making. Great leaders have something in them which inspires a whole people and makes them do great deeds.

The year you were born in—1919—was one of the great years of history when a great leader, with a heart full of love and sympathy for the poor and suffering, made his people write a noble and never-to-be-forgotten chapter of history. In the very month you were born, Lenin started his great Revolution which has changed the face of Russia and Siberia. And to-day in India another great leader, also full of love for all who suffer and passionately eager to help them, has inspired our people to great endeavour and noble sacrifice, so that they may again be free and the starving and the poor and the oppressed may have their burdens removed from them. Bapuji* lies in prison; but the magic of his message steals into the hearts of India's millions, and men and women, and even little children, come out of their little shells and become India's soldiers of freedom. In India to-day we are making history, and you and I are fortunate

* Mahatma Gandhi.

to see this happen before our eyes and to take some part ourselves in this great drama.

How shall we bear ourselves in this great movement? What part shall we play in it? I cannot say what part will fall to our lot; but, whatever it may be, let us remember that we can do nothing which may bring discredit to our cause or dishonour to our people. If we are to be India's soldiers we have India's honour in our keeping, and that honour is a sacred trust. Often we may be in doubt as to what to do. It is no easy matter to decide what is right and what is not. One little test I shall ask you to apply whenever you are in doubt. It may help you. Never do anything in secret or anything that you would wish to hide. For the desire to hide anything means that you are afraid, and fear is a bad thing and unworthy of you. Be brave, and all the rest follows. If you are brave, you will not fear and will not do anything of which you are ashamed. You know that in our great Freedom Movement, under Bapuji's leadership, there is no room for secrecy or hiding. We have nothing to hide. We are not afraid of what we do and what we say. We work in the sun and in the light. Even so in our private lives let us make friends with the sun and work in the light and do nothing secretly or furtively. Privacy, of course, we may have and should have, but that is a very different thing from secrecy. And if you do so, my dear, you will grow up a child of the light, unafraid and serene and unruffled, whatever may happen.

I have written to you a very long letter. And yet

there is so much I would like to tell you. How can a letter contain it?

You are fortunate, I have said, in being a witness to this great struggle for freedom that is going on in our country. You are also very fortunate in having a very brave and wonderful little woman for your Mummie, and if you are ever in doubt or in trouble you cannot have a better friend.

Good-bye, little one, and may you grow up into a brave soldier in India's service.

With all my love and good wishes.

8

THE LAST LETTER TO INDIRA*

WE have finished, my dear; the long story has ended. I need write no more, but the desire to end off with a kind of flourish induces me to write another letter—the Last Letter!

It was time I finished, for the end of my two-year term draws near. In three and thirty days from to-day I should be discharged, if indeed I am not released sooner, as the gaoler sometimes threatens to do. The full two years are not over yet, but I have received three and a half months' remission of my sentence, as all well-behaved prisoners do. For I am supposed to be a well-behaved prisoner, a reputation which I have certainly done nothing to deserve. So ends my sixth sentence, and I shall go out again into the wide world, but to what purpose? *A quoi bon?*—when most of my friends and comrades lie in gaol and the whole country seems a vast prison.

What a mountain of letters I have written! And what a lot of good *swadeshi*† ink I have spread out on *swadeshi* paper. Was it worth while, I wonder? Will all this paper and ink convey any message to you that will interest you? You will say "Yes," of course, for you

* For over two years, with a short break when he was out of prison, J. N. continued to write letters to his daughter from prison, giving her an outline of world history. The previous chapter is the first: this is the last of the series, written in August 1933.

† Home-made, that is, Indian made.

will feel that any other answer might hurt me, and you are too partial to me to take such a risk. But whether you care for them or not, you cannot grudge me the joy of having written them, day after day, during these two long years. It was winter when I came. Winter gave place to our brief spring, slain all too soon by the summer heat; and then when the ground was parched and dry and men and beasts panted for breath, came the monsoon with its bountiful supply of fresh and cool rain water. Autumn followed, and the sky was wonderfully clear and blue, and the afternoons were pleasant. The year's cycle was over, and again it began: winter and spring and summer and the rainy season. I have sat here, writing to you and thinking of you, and watched the seasons go by, and listened to the pit-a-pat of the rain on my barrack roof—

O doux bruit de la pluie,
Par terre et sur les toits!
Pour un cœur qui s'ennuie,
Oh! le chant de la pluie!*

Benjamin Disraeli, the great English statesman of the nineteenth century, has written that: "Other men condemned to exile and captivity, if they survive, despair; the man of letters may reckon those days as the sweetest of his life." He was writing about Hugo Grotius, a famous Dutch jurist and philosopher of the

* O soft sound of rain
On earth and on the roofs
For a heart that is pining
Oh! the song of the rain.

seventeenth century, who was condemned to imprisonment for life, but managed to escape after two years. He spent these two years in prison in philosophic and literary work. There have been many famous literary gaolbirds, the two best known perhaps being the Spaniard, Cervantes, who wrote *Don Quixote*, and the Englishman, John Bunyan, the author of *The Pilgrim's Progress.*

I am not a man of letters and I am not prepared to say that the many years I have spent in gaol have been the sweetest in my life, but I must say that reading and writing have helped me wonderfully to get through them. I am not a literary man, and I am not a historian; what indeed am I? I find it difficult to answer that question. I have been a dabbler in many things; I began with science at college and then took to the law, and, after developing various other interests in life, finally adopted the popular and widely practised profession of gaol-going in India!

You must not take what I have written in these letters as the final authority on any subject. A politician wants to have a say on every subject, and he always pretends to know much more than he actually does. He has to be watched carefully! These letters of mine are but superficial sketches joined together by a thin thread. I have rambled on, skipping centuries and many important happenings, and then pitching my tent for quite a long time on some event which interested me. As you will notice, my likes and dislikes are pretty obvious, and so also sometimes are my moods in gaol. I do not want you to take all this for granted; there may indeed be many errors in my accounts. A prison, with no libraries or reference books at hand, is not the most suitable place to write on historical subjects. I have had to rely very largely on the many note-books which I have accumulated since I began my visits to gaol twelve years ago. Many books have also come to me here; they have come and gone, for I could not collect a library here. I have shamelessly taken from these books facts and ideas; there is nothing original in what I have written. Perhaps occasionally you may find my letters difficult to follow; skip those parts, do not mind them. The grown-up in me got the better of me sometimes and I wrote as I should not have done.

I have given you the barest outline; this is not history; they are just fleeting glimpses of our long past. If history interests you, if you feel some of the fascination of history, you will find your way to many books which will help you to unravel the threads of past ages. But reading books alone will not help. If you would know the past you must look upon it with sympathy and with understanding. To understand a person who lived long ago, you will have to understand his environment, the conditions under which he lived, the ideas that filled his mind. It is absurd for us to judge of past people as if they lived now and thought as we do. There is no one to defend slavery to-day, and yet the great Plato held that slavery was essential. Within recent times scores of thousands of lives were given in an effort to retain slavery in the United States. We cannot judge the past from the standards of the present. Everyone will willingly admit this. But everyone will not admit the equally absurd habit of judging the present by the standards of the past. The various religions have especially helped in petrifying old beliefs and faiths and customs, which may have had some use in the age and country of their birth, but which are singularly unsuitable in our present age.

If, then, you look upon past history with the eye of sympathy, the dry bones will fill up with flesh and blood, and you will see a mighty procession of living men and women and children in every age and every clime, different from us and yet very like us, with much the same human virtues and human failings. History is not a magic show, but there is plenty of magic in it for those who have eyes to see.

Innumerable pictures from the gallery of history crowd our minds. Egypt—Babylon—Nineveh—the old Indian civilizations—the coming of the Aryans to India and their spreading out over Europe and Asia—the wonderful record of Chinese culture—Knossos and Greece—Imperial Rome and Byzantium—the triumphant march of the Arabs across two continents—the renascence of Indian culture and its decay—the little known Maya and Aztec civilizations of America—the vast conquests of the Mongols—the Middle Ages in Europe with their wonderful Gothic cathedrals—the coming of Islam to India and the Mughal Empire—the Renaissance of learning and art in Western Europe—the discovery of America and the sea routes to the East—the beginnings of Western aggression in the East—the coming of the big machine and the development of capitalism—the spread of industrialism and European domination and imperialism—and the wonders of science in the modern world.

Great Empires have risen and fallen and been forgotten by man for thousands of years, till their remains were dug up again by patient explorers from under the sands that covered them. And yet many an idea, many a fancy has survived and proved stronger and more persistent than the Empire.

> Egypt's might is tumbled down
> Down a-down the deeps of thought;
> Greece is fallen and Troy town,
> Glorious Rome hath lost her crown,
> Venice' pride is nought.
> But the dreams their children dreamed
> Fleeting, unsubstantial, vain,
> Shadowy as the shadows seemed,
> Airy nothing, as they deemed,
> These remain.

So sings Mary Coleridge.

The past brings us many gifts; indeed, all that we have to-day of culture, civilization, science, or knowledge of some aspects of the truth, is a gift of the distant or recent past to us. It is right that we acknowledge our obligation to the past. But the past does not exhaust our duty or obligation. We owe a duty to the future also and perhaps that obligation is even greater than the one we owe to the past. For the past is past and done with, we cannot change it; the future is yet to come, and perhaps we may be able to shape it a little.

If the past has given us some part of the truth, the future also hides many aspects of the truth and invites us to search for it. But often the past is jealous of the future and holds us in a terrible grip, and we have to struggle with it to get free to face and advance towards the future.

History, it is said, has many lessons to teach us; and there is another saying that history never repeats itself. Both are true, for we cannot learn anything from it by slavishly trying to copy it, or by expecting it to repeat itself or remain stagnant; but we can learn something from it by prying behind it and trying to discover the forces that move it. Even so what we get is seldom a straight answer. "History," says Karl Marx, "has no other way of answering old questions than by putting new ones."

The old days were days of faith; blind, unquestioning faith. The wonderful temples and mosques and cathedrals of past centuries could never have been built but for the overpowering faith of the architects and builders and people generally. The very stones they reverently put one on top of the other, or carved in beautiful designs, tell us of this faith. The old temple spire, the mosque with its slender minarets, the Gothic cathedral—all of them pointing upward with an amazing intensity of devotion, as if offering a prayer in stone or marble to the sky above—thrill us even now, though we may be lacking in that faith of old of which they are the embodiments. But the days of that faith are gone, and gone with them is that magic touch in stone. Thousands of temples and mosques and cathedrals continue to be built, but they lack the spirit that made them live during the Middle Ages. There is little difference between them and the commercial offices which are so representative of our age.

Our age is a different one; it is an age of disillusion, of doubt and uncertainty and questioning. We can no longer accept many of the ancient beliefs and customs; we have no more faith in them, in Asia or in Europe or America. So we search for new ways, new aspects of the truth more in harmony with our environment. And we question each other and debate and quarrel and evolve any number of "isms" and philosophies. As in the days of Socrates, we live in an age of questioning, but that questioning is not confined to a city like Athens; it is world-wide.

Sometimes the injustice, the unhappiness, the brutality of the world oppress us and darken our minds, and we see no way out. With Matthew Arnold, we feel that there is no hope in this world, and all we can do is to be true to one another.

> For the world which seems
> To lie before us, like a land of dreams,
> So various, so beautiful, so new,
> Hath really neither joy, nor love, nor light,
> Nor certitude, nor peace, nor help for pain;
> And we are here, as on a darkling plain
> Swept with confused alarms of struggle and flight,
> Where ignorant armies clash by night.

And yet if we take such a dismal view we have not learnt aright the lesson of life or of history. For history teaches us of growth and progress and of the possibility of an infinite advance for man. And life is rich and varied, and though it has many swamps and marshes and muddy places, it has also the great sea, and the mountains, and snow, and glaciers, and wonderful star-lit nights (especially in gaol!), and the love of family and friends, and the comradeship of workers in a common cause, and music, and books, and the Empire of ideas. So that each one of us may well say:

> Lord, though I lived on earth, the child of earth,
> Yet was I fathered by the starry sky.

It is easy to admire the beauties of the universe and to live in a world of thought and imagination. But to try to escape in this way from the unhappiness of others, caring little what happens to them, is no sign of courage or fellow-feeling. Thought, in order to justify itself, must lead to action. "Action is the end of thought," says our friend Romain Rolland, "All thought which does not look towards action is an abortion and a treachery. If then we are the servants of thought we must be the servants of action."

People avoid action often because they are afraid of the consequences, for action means risk and danger. Danger seems terrible from a distance; it is not so bad if you have a close look at it. And often it is a pleasant companion, adding to the zest and delight of life. The ordinary course of life becomes dull at times, and we take too many things for granted and have no joy in them. And yet how we appreciate these common things of life when we have lived without them for a while! Many people go up high mountains and risk life and limb for the joy of the climb and the exhilaration that comes from a difficulty surmounted, a danger overcome; and because of the danger that hovers all around them, their perceptions get keener, their joy of the life which hangs by a thread, the more intense.

All of us have our choice of living in the valleys below with their unhealthy mists and fogs, but giving a measure of bodily security; or of climbing the high mountains, with risk and danger for companions, to breathe the pure air above, and take joy in the distant views, and welcome the rising sun.

I have given you many quotations and extracts from poets and others in this letter. I shall finish up with one more. It is from the *Gitanjali*; it is a poem, or prayer, by Rabindra Nath Tagore:

Where the mind is without fear and the head is held high;
Where knowledge is free;
Where the world has not been broken up into fragments by
    narrow domestic walls;
Where words come out from the depth of truth;
Where tireless striving stretches its arms towards perfection;
Where the clear stream of reason has not lost its way into
    the dreary desert sand of dead habit;
Where the mind is led forward by thee into ever-widening
    thought and action—
Into that heaven of freedom, my Father, let my country
    awake.

We have finished, carissima, and this last letter ends. The last letter! Certainly not! I shall write you many more. But this series ends, and so

*Tāmam Shud!**

* A Persian expression: "It is finished."

9

MAHATMA GANDHI*

MR. SOUMYANDRANATH TAGORE is one of our young comrades in India for whom I have the greatest respect. Ardent, clear-headed, and devoted to the cause of the freedom of the masses, anything that he says or writes must deserve attention. But I have seen with great regret the criticism of Gandhi which he has written in a recent book. All legitimate criticism is to be welcomed, for it helps us to get at the truth, and no personality, however great, should be above this criticism. But it seems to me that Mr. Tagore has done an injustice to himself and has failed to grasp many of the underlying factors of the Indian situation in his eagerness to paint Gandhi as a reactionary force in every way. It is not possible for me in these lines to consider many of Mr. Tagore's statements which I think are wrong. But, as one who has differed from Gandhi in many important matters and yet co-operated with him in a large measure, I should like to express my disagreement with Mr. Tagore's basic analysis of Gandhi.

It should be remembered that the nationalist movement in India, like all nationalist movements, was essentially a bourgeois movement. It represented the

* This article, which was published in *L'Europe* early in 1936, was written in reply to attacks on Mr. Gandhi which Mr. Soumyandranath Tagore had recently published in France.

natural historical stage of development, and to consider it or to criticize it as a working-class movement is wrong. Gandhi represented that movement and the Indian masses in relation to that movement to a supreme degree, and he became the voice of the Indian people to that extent. He functioned inevitably within the orbit of nationalist ideology, but the dominating passion that consumed him was a desire to raise the masses. In this respect he was always ahead of the nationalist movement, and he gradually made it, within the limits of its own ideology, turn in this direction. Economic events in India and the world powerfully pushed Indian nationalism towards vital social changes, and to-day it hovers, somewhat undecided, on the brink of a new social ideology.

But the main contribution of Gandhi to India and the Indian masses has been through the powerful movements which he launched through the National Congress. Through nation-wide action he sought to mould the millions, and largely succeeded in doing so, and changing them from a demoralized, timid, and hopeless mass, bullied and crushed by every dominant interest, and incapable of resistance, into a people with self-respect and self-reliance, resisting tyranny, and capable of united action and sacrifice for a larger cause. He made them think of political and economic issues, and every village and every bazaar hummed with argument and debate on the new ideas and hopes that filled the people. That was an amazing psychological change. The time was ripe for it, of course, and circumstances and world conditions worked for this change. But a great leader is necessary to take advantage of circumstances and conditions. Gandhi was that leader, and he released many of the bonds that imprisoned and disabled our minds, and none of us who experienced it can ever forget that great feeling of release and exhilaration that came over the Indian people. Gandhi has played a revolutionary role in India of the greatest importance because he knew how to make the most of the objective conditions and could reach the heart of the masses; while groups with a more advanced ideology functioned largely in the air because they did not fit in with those conditions and could therefore not evoke any substantial response from the masses.

To call Gandhi an ally of British imperialism is the veriest nonsense which can only evoke a smile. The answer to that charge can best be given by the British Government and by British imperialists, who have all along considered him their most dangerous opponent. They have tried to suppress him and oppose him in every way, and the measure of their reaction to him and to the National Congress is the wide-flung and intensive repression that is going on in India.

It is perfectly true that Gandhi, functioning in the nationalist plane, does not think in terms of the conflict of classes, and tries to compose their differences. But the action he has indulged in and taught the people has inevitably raised mass consciousness tremendously and made social issues vital. And his insistence on the raising of the masses at the cost, wherever necessary, of vested interests has given a strong orientation to the national movement in favour of the masses.

Essentially, the Congress under Gandhi's leadership has been a joint and anti-imperialist front. Mr. Tagore in his book does not believe in the desirability of such a united front. But I should be surprised if he has not changed his opinion since he wrote his book, for, as everyone knows, the policy of the Comintern and the Communist parties in different countries has undergone a great change in recent months in favour of a united front. In France there is the Front Populaire, in England the Communist Party wants to co-operate with the Labour Party, and in the colonial countries there is the definite attempt at co-operation with nationalist movements. In India itself, so far as I know, they are in favour of a joint anti-imperialist front.

Gandhi and the Congress must be judged by the policies they pursue and the action they indulge in. But behind this, personality counts and colours those policies and activities. In the case of a very exceptional person like Gandhi the question of personality becomes especially important in order to understand and appraise him. An English journalist, Mr. George Slocombe, who has had a wide experience of men prominent and otherwise in public affairs all over the world, has referred to Gandhi in a recent book of his, and the passage is interesting and worth quoting. He says: "I have never met any man more utterly honest, more transparently sincere, less given to egotism, self-conscious pride, opportunism, and ambition which are found in greater or less degree in all the other great political figures of the world." An English journalist's opinion need not carry much weight with us, nor does the sincerity of a person excuse a wrong policy or mistaken ideas. But as it happens, that opinion is shared by millions in India, and it is very superficial criticism to dispose of such a unique and outstanding personality by cheap and well-worn phrases which are applied indiscriminately to the average politician. We in India have often differed from Gandhi, we differ from him still in many ways, and sometimes we may follow different paths, but it has been the greatest privilege of our lives to work with him and under him for a great cause. To us he has represented the spirit and honour of India, the yearning of her sorrowing millions to be rid of their innumerable burdens, and an insult to him by the British Government or others has been an insult to India and her people.

10

A LETTER TO AN ENGLISHMAN*

PART I.—IMPERIALISM AND SOCIALISM

I ENTIRELY agree with you that we are in the midst of one of the most creative and changing epochs in human history. It does seem that we have reached an end of an era and are on the threshold of another. I also agree that the two ideals which are moving most intelligent and sensitive persons are: the ending of the present anarchy of sovereign States, with their hatreds, fears, and conflicts, and the creation of a world order; and the socialistic ideal, aiming at "a system whereby the earth and its fruits will be exploited for the benefit of all members of the community in proportion for the services they render to it, and not according to the accident of property ownership." The League of Nations, you say, represents the former ideal. I think this is so in so far as it represents a widespread sentiment. In actual practice, however, it hardly functions that way, and it represents the policies of certain Great Powers who have no intention of giving up their privileged positions, or their absolute

* This letter, written in reply to a letter sent to Mr. Nehru at Badenweiler in January 1936, is published here with the consent of the recipient.

sovereignty, and who endeavour to utilize the League to make the world safe for themselves.

Another question arises. Even if the people behind the League honestly desired the ending of the anarchy of sovereign States, or were pushed by popular opinion in that direction, could they succeed in that objective without changing fundamentally the social order—without, in other words, accepting Socialism? Of course they would have to shed their imperialism. The League to-day does not look beyond the present capitalistic system; indeed, it does not even contemplate an ending of imperialism. It is essentially based on the *status quo* and its chief function is to preserve it. In practice, therefore, it is actually a hindrance to the realization of the very ideal which many people think it represents. If it is true, as I believe it is, that imperialism and the anarchy of sovereign States are inevitable developments of the present phase of capitalism, then it follows that you cannot get rid of the former without also getting rid of the latter. But in practice the League has little to do with its supposed ideals, and even puts difficulties in the way of their realization; but even its ideals, by themselves, are such that they lead to a blind alley. It is not surprising that it finds itself frequently involved in hopeless contradictions. It simply cannot go ahead on the basis of the *status quo* because the root of the trouble is that *status quo* both in its imperialist and social aspects. It is right and proper that the League should condemn Italian aggression in Abyssinia and try to curb it, but the very system which it protects and seeks to perpetuate inevitably leads to that aggression. There is no valid answer for an imperialist to Mussolini's taunt that he is doing what other imperialist powers have done before, and are doing now, though not in his particularly blatant way. It does seem rather illogical to condemn Italian bombing in East Africa, and maintain a dignified silence about British bombing in the North-West Frontier of India.

You yourself are of opinion that the achievement of the end is not likely to be by the method of the Covenant of the League. The League, therefore, offers little hope, except in so far as it represents a vague but widespread sentiment in favour of world order and peace. It helps sometimes in mobilizing that sentiment and in postponing conflict.

The two ideals you have mentioned run into each other, and I do not think they can be separated. The second ideal, of Socialism, indeed, includes the first, and it may be said that real world order and peace will only come when Socialism is realized on a world scale. It is perfectly true, as you say, that real Socialism involves a profound transformation of the deeper habits of opinion and of character and this inevitably takes time. Under favourable circumstances, and with the goodwill of a large number of people concerned, these changes may be brought about within a generation. But as things are, instead of that goodwill we have the fiercest opposition and ill will, and it is therefore likely that the period will be a much longer one. The main question for us to consider is how to create an environment and circumstances under which these deeper changes can take place. Only that will be a real step in the right direction. Under present circumstances the environment is against us, and instead of lessening our mutual hatreds and selfishness and acquisitiveness, which lead to conflict, actually encourages these evil traits. It is true that in spite of these grave disadvantages some progress is made, and some of us at least begin to challenge our old habits and opinions. But the process is very slow, and it is almost counterbalanced by the growth of contrary tendencies.

Capitalism has stimulated acquisitiveness and these deeper instincts which we want to get rid of now. It did much good also in its earlier stages, and by raising production greatly increased the standard of living. In other ways, too, it served a useful purpose, and it was certainly an improvement on the stage that preceded it. But it seems to have outlived its utility, and to-day it not only bars all progress in a socialistic direction, but encourages many undesirable habits and instincts in us. I do not see how we can move along socialistic lines in a society which is based on acquisitiveness, and in which the profit motive is the dominant urge. It thus becomes necessary to change the basis of this acquisitive society, and to remove the profit motive, as far as we can, in order to develop new and more desirable habits and ways of thinking. That involves a complete change-over from the capitalist system.

It is true, as you state, that the capitalist system has not created international anarchy; it merely succeeded to it. It has in the past removed or lessened actual civil war within the State, but it has intensified the conflict of classes, which has grown to such an extent as to threaten civil war in the future. In the international sphere it has perpetuated anarchy on a bigger scale, and, instead of petty local wars, it has brought about vast and terrible national conflicts. And so, though it does not create this anarchy, it inevitably increases it, and cannot put an end to it unless it puts an end to itself. It has produced the modern imperialisms which not only crush and exploit large parts of the earth's surface and vast numbers of people, but also come into continual conflict with each other.

It may be that Marx overstates the case for the materialist or economic interpretation of history. Perhaps he did so for the simple reason that it had been largely ignored, or at any rate very much understated till then. But Marx never denied the influence of other factors on the shaping of events. He laid the greatest stress on one—the economic factor. Whether that stress was a little overdone does not make much difference. The fact remains, I think, that his interpretation of history is the only one which does explain history to some extent and give it meaning. It helps us to understand the present, and it is quite remarkable how many of his predictions have come true.

How will Socialism come? You say that it is not likely to be achieved by the universal nationalization of the instruments of production and distribution. Must it not involve the ending of the profit and acquisitive motive and the replacement of it by a communal and co-operative motive? And does it not involve the building up of a new civilization on a different basis from that of the present? It may be that a great deal of private initiative is left; in some matters, cultural, etc., it must be left. But in all that counts, in a material sense, nationalization of the instruments of production and distribution seems to be inevitable. There may be half-way houses to it, but one can hardly have two contradictory and conflicting processes going on side by side. The choice must be made, and for one who aims at Socialism there can only be one choice.

I think it is possible, in theory, to establish Socialism by democratic means, provided of course the full democratic process is available. In practice, however, there are likely to be very great difficulties, because the opponents of Socialism will reject the democratic method when they see their power threatened. The rejection of democracy does not, or should not, come from the Socialist side, but from the other. That of course is Fascism. How is this to be avoided? The democratic method has many triumphs to its credit, but I do not know that it has yet succeeded in resolving a conflict about the very basic structure of the State or of society. When this question arises, the group or class which controls the State-power does not voluntarily give it up because the majority demands it. We have seen enough examples of it in post-war Europe and the decline of democracy itself. Obviously no Socialist transformation can be brought about without the goodwill, or at least the passive acquiescence, of the great majority.

PART II.—BRITAIN AND INDIA

Coming to Britain and India, I find a large number of assumptions in your letter which I think have little justification. As I do not agree with many of your premises, I also find myself in disagreement with some of your conclusions. You say that "Britain is shedding the old imperialism and is actively concerned with trying to find the way to prevent the anarchy involved in universal national self-determination from ending in fresh wars, or in a new deluge of imperialism." I am afraid I entirely fail to see that Britain is acting in this role. I do not see any shedding of the old imperialism, but only repeated and strenuous attempts to hold on to it, and to strengthen it, though a new façade is presented to the public view in some instances. Britain certainly does not want fresh wars. She is a satisfied and a surfeited Power. Why should she risk what she has got? She wants to maintain the *status quo* which is eminently to her advantage. She dislikes new imperialisms because they conflict with her old imperialism, and not because of any dislike of imperialism itself.

You refer also to the "constitutional road" in India. What exactly is this constitutional road? I can understand constitutional activities where there is a democratic constitution, but where there is no such thing constitutional methods have no meaning. The word constitutional then simply means legal, and legal simply means in accordance with the wishes of an autocratic executive which can make laws and issue decrees and ordinances regardless of public opinion. What is the constitutional method in Germany or Italy to-day? What was this method in the India of the nineteenth century or of the early twentieth century, or even now? There was no possibility of bringing about a change in India then (or now) through any constitutional apparatus which the people of India could sufficiently influence. They could only beg or revolt. The mere fact that it is impossible for the great majority of the people of India to make their will effective shows that they have no constitutional way open to them. They can either submit to something they dislike intensely, or adopt other than so-called constitutional methods. Such methods may be wise or unwise, under the particular circumstances, but the question of their being constitutional or not does not arise.

Most of us, I suppose, are unable to get rid of our particular national bias, and often ignore the beam in our own eyes. I realize that I must be subject to this, especially when I consider the relation of Britain and India. You will allow for that. Nevertheless I must say that nothing astonishes me so much as the way the British people manage to combine their material interests with their moral fervour; how they proceed on the irrebuttable presumption that they are always doing good to the world and acting from the highest motives, and trouble and conflict and difficulty are caused by the obstinacy and evil-mindedness of others. That presumption, as you know, is not universally accepted, and in Europe and America and Asia it is the subject of humorous comment. In India especially we may be forgiven if we reject it utterly after our experience of British rule in the past and present. To talk of democracy and constitutionalism in India, in the face of what has happened and is happening there, seems to me to distort utterly the significance of these terms. Ruling powers and ruling classes have not been known in history to abdicate willingly. And if the teaching of history was not enough, we in India have had enough experience of hard facts.

It is true, I think, that the British ruling classes possess a certain instinct for adaptability, but when the very basis of their power is challenged there is little room for superficial adaptation. For anyone to imagine that the British Government or Parliament are kindly trustees for Indian freedom and are beneficently presiding over its development seems to me one of the most extraordinary of delusions. I believe there are many Britishers who feel kindly towards India and her people, and would like to see India free, but they count for little in the shaping of policy, and even they, or most of them, think in terms of Indian freedom fitting in with British desires and interests. More freedom, greater responsibility, will come to us, we are told, as we show our fitness for it, and the test of this is how far we fit in with the British scheme of things. One almost feels like suggesting to our mentors and well-wishers in England to renew their acquaintance with *Æsop's Fables*, and especially to read afresh the story of the wolf and the lamb.

It is perfectly true that in politics, as in most other things, we cannot start with a clean slate. It is also true that life is often too complex for human logic. We have to take things as they are, whether we like them or not, and to reconcile our idealism with them. But we must move in the right direction. This means, according to you, first of all the preservation of the unity of India and then the elimination of communalism, the control and gradual divesting of vested interests, and the raising of the standard of living of the people, the development of a true Indian army, and the training of the youth of India in constructive practical work required in a democratic State. Beyond all this lies the socialistic ideal, and the general background must be such as to develop those deeper instincts and habits which are necessary for the real working of this ideal.

I suppose many of us would agree with that statement so far as it goes, though we may word it differently, and add to it, and stress some points more than others. I agree with you also that the political phase comes first; indeed, without that phase there is no other phase. It may be accompanied by social changes, or followed soon after by them. Personally, I am perfectly prepared to accept political democracy only, in the hope that this will lead to social democracy. Political democracy is only the way to the goal, and is not the final objective. The real demand for it comes from a desire, sometimes unconscious, for economic changes. If these changes do not follow soon enough the political structure is likely to be unstable. I am inclined to think that in India, circumstanced as she is to-day, the need for economic change is urgent, and a vital political change will inevitably be accompanied or followed by substantial economic changes. In any event the political change should be such as to facilitate these social changes. If it becomes a barrier to them then it is not a desirable change, or one worth having.

I am not aware of any responsible Indian who thinks in terms other than the unity of India. That is an essential article of our political faith and anything that we do has that for its goal. That unity, I agree, is likely to be a federal unity, but that does not mean of course anything like the federation of the new Act. That unity also is not the unity of subjection under a common yoke. It is possible that a period of chaos might result in disunity and the formation of separate States in India, but that danger seems to me very unreal. The tendency to unity is too strong all over the country.

The disruptive factors are according to you: religion, race, and language. I do not see the importance of race. Race in India became intertwined with religion, and partly took the shape of caste. Hindus and Moslems do not form different races; they are essentially the same amalgam of races. Thus, though there are various races, they run into one another and on the whole form, a definite unit, racially and culturally The so-called hundreds of languages of India are a favourite subject for our critics, who usually have little acquaintance with any of them. As a matter of fact India is linguistically singularly well knit, and it is only due to the absence of popular education that numerous dialects have grown. There are ten major languages of India which cover the entire country, except for some small tracts. These belong to the two groups—Indo-Aryan and Dravidian—and between the two there is the common background of Sanskrit. Of the Indo-Aryan languages, I suppose you know that Hindustani with its various dialects accounts for over 120,000,000 of people, and it is spreading. The other Indo-Aryan languages—Bengali, Gujerati and Marathi—are very closely allied to it. I am sure that whatever other difficulties we may have to face in the way of Indian unity, the language question will not be a major difficulty.

You compare the state of religion in India with that of Europe at the time of the Renaissance and the Reformation. It is true that the people of India have a definite religious outlook which is comparable to the outlook in Europe during the Middle Ages. Still your comparison does not go below the surface. India has never known in the whole course of her long history the religious strife that has soaked Europe in blood. The whole background of Indian religion, culture, and philosophy was one of tolerance, and even encouragement of other beliefs. Some conflict arose when Islam came, but even that was far more political than religious, although stress is always laid on the religious side. It was the conflict between the conquerors and the conquered. In spite of recent developments I cannot easily envisage religious conflict in India on any substantial scale. The communalism of to-day is essentially political, economic, and middle-class. I imagine (but I say so without personal knowledge) that the religious bitterness in Ulster to-day is far more deep-seated than anywhere in India. It is a fact that one must never forget that communalism in India is a latter-day phenomenon which has grown up before our eyes. That does not lessen its significance, and we may not ignore it, for it is at present a tremendous obstacle in our way and is likely to interfere with our future progress. And yet I think it is overrated and overemphasized; it does not fundamentally affect the masses, although sometimes their passions are roused. With the coming of social issues to the forefront it is bound to recede into the background. Examine the communal demands of the extreme communalists and you will find that not a single one of them has the slightest reference to the masses. These communal leaders of all groups are terribly afraid of social and economic questions, and it is interesting to find them joining hands in their opposition to social progress.

British rule in India has inevitably helped in creating political unity in the country. The mere fact of common subjection was bound to result in a common desire to be rid of it. It must be remembered—a fact that is not sufficiently realized—that throughout history there has been a quite extraordinary sense of cultural and geographical unity in India, and the desire for political unity was bound to grow under modern conditions of transport and communication. Throughout the British period, however, there has been an attempt on the part of the ruling power, partly conscious and deliberate, partly unconscious, to retard this unity. That, of course, was only to be expected, for that has been the invariable policy of all empires and ruling groups. It is interesting to read the frank expressions of opinion of high officers in India during the nineteenth century. The problem was then not very urgent, but with the growth of the nationalist movement, and especially during the last thirty years, it became acute. The reaction of the British Government was to devise new methods for creating and, if possible, perpetuating these divisions. Obviously no one can say that there was not an inherent tendency towards division in India, and with the prospect of the approach of political power, this was likely to grow. It was possible to adopt a policy to tone down this tendency; it was also possible to accentuate it. The Government adopted the latter policy and encouraged in every way every fissiparous tendency in the country. It is not possible for them or for anyone to stop the historical growth of the people, but they can and they have put checks and obstructions in the way. And the latest and most important of these are in the new Act. You commend this Act because it symbolizes the unity of India. As a matter of fact it is the very reverse; it is the prelude (if it is not combated) of greater disunity. It divides up India into religious and numerous other compartments, preserves large parts of it as feudal enclaves which cannot be touched, but which can influence other parts, and checks the growth of healthy political parties on social and economic issues, which you consider "the most important and urgent need in India to-day."

The policy of the British Government on social issues is equally marked. Far from looking towards any form of Socialism or control or divesting of vested interests, it has deliberately protected numerous vested interests, created fresh ones, and invariably sided with the political, social, and religious reactionaries in India. The new Act is again the culmination of this policy, and at no time before have these vested interests and obscurantists and reactionaries had so much power as they will have under the new federal India. The Act legally bars the door to that social progress which, according to you, should be our goal, by protecting and entrenching these vested interests, foreign and Indian. Even small measures of social reform are hardly within reach, as a very great part of the financial resources of the State are mortgaged and ear-marked for the maintenance of vested interests.

Every country to-day has to put up a stiff fight against the forces of reaction and evil. India is no exception to the rule. The tragedy of the situation is that the British people, without being conscious of it, stand to-day through their Parliament and officials entirely on the side of the forces of evil in India. What they would not tolerate for an instant in their own country, they encourage in India. You mention the great name of Abraham Lincoln, and remind me of the great importance he attached to the Union. Presumably you think that the British Government, in trying to suppress the Congress movement, was actuated by the same noble motive of maintaining the unity of India in the face of disruptive forces. I do not quite see how the unity of India was threatened by that movement—indeed I think that that movement or some similar movement alone can bring about an organic unity in the country, and the British Government's activities push us in a contrary direction. But apart from this, do you not think that the comparison of Lincoln with the attempt of an imperialist power to crush the freedom movement in a country subject to it is very far-fetched?

You want to eradicate undesirable and selfish habits and instincts in the people. Do you think that the British in India are helping in this direction? Quite apart from their support of the reactionary elements, the background of British rule is worth considering. It is, of course, based on an extreme form of widespread violence, and the only sanction is fear. It suppresses the usual liberties which are supposed to be essential to the growth of a people; it crushes the adventurous, the brave, the sensitive types, and encourages the timid, the opportunist and time-serving, the sneak and the bully. It surrounds itself with a vast army of spies and informers and *agents provocateurs*. Is this the atmosphere in which the more desirable virtues grow or democratic institutions flourish?

You ask me whether the Congress could at any time

have established a liberal constitution for all India by consent, except by making in fundamentals the same kind of concessions to communalism, to the Princes, and to property. That presumes that the present Act establishes a liberal constitution by consent. If this constitution is a liberal one it is difficult for me to imagine what an illiberal constitution can be like, and as for consent, I doubt that anything that the British Government have ever done in India has been quite so much resented and disapproved of as the new Act. Incidentally, the measures to obtain the necessary consent involved the fiercest repression all over the country, and even now, as a prelude to the enforcement of the Act, all-India and provincial laws suppressing all kinds of civil liberty have been passed. To talk of consent under these circumstances does seem most extraordinary. There is an amazing amount of misconception about this in England. If the problem has to be faced the dominant facts cannot be ignored.

It is true that the Government has succeeded in making some arrangement with the Princes and with various minority groups, but even these groups are highly dissatisfied except, to some extent, with the minor arrangements affecting their representation. Take the principal minority, the Moslems. No one can say that the aristocratic, semi-feudal, and other hand-picked Moslem members of the Round Table Conference represented the Moslem masses. You may be surprised to know that the Congress has still considerable Moslem backing.

Could the Congress have done better? I have no doubt that the nationalist movement, of which the Congress is the symbol and the principal standard-bearer, could have done infinitely better. The Congress is of course a bourgeois organization (I wish it were more socialistic), and therefore the property qualification would not have arisen in acute form at this stage. The communal question would have had to be faced and, I think, solved for the time being at least with a large measure of consent. Probably some degree of communalism would have remained to begin with, but far less than what we are presented with under the new Act. What is more important—circumstances would have been created for the elimination of communalism in the near future and for growth along social lines; and the land problem would have been tackled. The real difficulties would have been two: the vested interests of the British Government and the City of London, and the Princes. The former represent the crux of the question, all else is really secondary. The Princes would, under the circumstances, have adapted themselves to a considerable extent to the new situation, and the Congress, constituted as it is to-day, would have given them a long enough rope. The pressure of public opinion, including that of their own subjects, would have been too great for them to resist. Probably some temporary arrangement might have been made with the Indian States to begin with to enable this public opinion to come into play and shape developments. Presuming of course that the British Government is not there to back up the undiluted autocracy of the Princes, there is little doubt that the States would gradually fall into line. No question of civil conflict need have arisen.

All this would have been very far from what I desire, but it would at least have been a definite political and democratic step in the right direction. In the framing of a constitution or a political structure it is manifestly impossible to get everyone concerned to agree. One tries to have the maximum agreement, and the others who do not agree either fall into line according to democratic procedure, or have to be pressed or coerced into doing so. The British Government, representing the autocratic and authoritarian tradition, and chiefly bent on preserving their own interests, tried to win the consent of the Princes and some other reactionary elements, and coerced the vast majority of the people. The Congress would have inevitably functioned differently.

All this is of course airy talk without substance, for it ignores the principal factor—the British Government.

There is another consideration which deserves notice. The Congress, under Mr. Gandhi's leadership, has laid great stress on non-violence and the conversion of the adversary rather than his coercion. Quite apart from the metaphysical aspects of this doctrine and its feasibility or otherwise in the final sense, there can be no doubt that this has created a powerful feeling against civil conflict and in favour of attempting to win over the various groups in India. That is a factor of great value to us in preserving the unity of India and in toning down opposition.

People discuss the non-co-operation and civil disobedience movements in terms of constitutional action or otherwise. I have referred to this aspect earlier. May I put to you how they have always impressed themselves on me? Of course these movements exercised tremendous pressure on the British Government and shook the Government machinery. But the real importance, to my mind, lay in the effect they had on our own people, and especially the village masses. Poverty and a long period of autocratic rule, with its inevitable atmosphere of coercion and fear, had thoroughly demoralized and degraded them. They had hardly any of the virtues that are necessary for citizenship; they were cuffed and bullied by every petty official, tax collector, policeman, landlord's agent; they were utterly lacking in courage or the capacity for united action or resistance to oppression; they sneaked and told tales against each other; and when life became too hard they sought an escape from it in death. It was all very depressing and deplorable, and yet one could hardly blame them for it; they were the victims of all-powerful circumstances. Non-co-operation dragged them out of this mire and gave them self-respect and self-reliance. They developed the habit of co-operative action; they acted courageously, and did not submit so easily to unjust oppression; their outlook widened, and they began to think a little in terms of India as a whole; they discussed political and economic questions (crudely, no doubt) in their bazaars and meeting-places. The lower middle class was affected in the same way,, but the change in the masses was the most significant. It was a remarkable transformation, and the Congress under Gandhi's leadership must have the credit for it. It was something far more important than constitutions and the structure of governments. It was the foundation on which alone a stable structure or constitution could be built up.

All this of course involved a cataclysmic upheaval of Indian life. Usually in other countries this has involved a vast amount of violence and hatred. And yet in India, thanks to Mahatma Gandhi, there was, relatively speaking, exceedingly little of this. We developed many of the virtues of war without its terrible evils, And the real organic unity of India was brought far nearer than it had ever been. Even the religious and communal differences toned down. You know that the most vital question that affects rural India—which means 85 per cent of India—is the land question. Any such upheaval in another country, together with the terrible economic depression, would have resulted there in *jacqueries*. It is extraordinary that India escaped them. That was not because of Government repression, but because of Gandhi's teaching and the message of the Congress.

Congress thus released all the live forces in the country and suppressed the evil and disruptive tendencies. It did so in a peaceful, disciplined, and as civilized way as was possible under the circumstances, though inevitably there were risks in such a mass release. How did the Government react? You know that well enough. By trying to crush those live and virile forces and encouraging all the evil and disruptive tendencies, and doing so in the most uncivilized way. The British Government has functioned in a purely Fascist way during the past six years, and the only difference has been that it did not take open pride in this fact as the Fascist countries do.

This letter has become terribly long, and I do not want now to consider the new Constitution Act in detail. That is hardly necessary, for the Act has been analysed and criticized by a host of persons in India holding all sorts of opinions, but agreeing in one thing —their utter disapproval of the Act. Very recently one of the most eminent leaders of the Indian Liberals described the new Constitution privately as "The quintessence of the most venomous opposition to all our national aspirations." Is it not remarkable that even our moderate politicians should think so, and yet you, with all your broad sympathy for Indian aspirations, should approve of it and say that it "involves the transfer of the citadel of power in India to Indian hands"? Is the gulf between our ways of thinking so vast? Why is it so? It almost becomes more of a problem in psychology than in politics or economics.

The psychological aspect is after all very important. Is it realized in England what the past few years have meant to India? How the attempt to crush human dignity and decency, the injuries to the soul more even than to the body, have left a lasting impress on the Indian people? Never have I realized so well how a tyrannical use of power degrades those who use it as well as those who suffer from it. How can we forget it without forgetting everything that is decent and honourable? How can we forget it when it continues from day to day? Is this the prelude to freedom and the transfer of the citadel of power?

People react in different ways to oppression. Some are broken, others harden. We have both kinds in India as elsewhere. Many of us cannot desert our colleagues, who suffer in prison or otherwise, whatever the consequences might be to our individual selves. Many of us cannot tolerate an insult to Gandhi, whether we differ from him or not, for Gandhi represents to us the honour of India. No one in his senses likes conflict and suffering and the way of catastrophe. The Indian national movement has done all in its power to avoid this way, without at the same time giving up the very basis of its existence. But it is the British Government that has proceeded along that path and made a peaceful solution more and more difficult. If it imagines that by merely persisting in this direction it will succeed, it seems to have strangely misread both the lesson of history and the present temper of the Indian people. If catastrophe is to be avoided, it will have to be for the British Government to retrace its steps.

II

INDIA AND THE WORLD*

FACED by repeated crises and engrossed in their domestic troubles, it is not surprising that the people of the West should pay little attention to India. A few may feel drawn to the rich past of India and admire her ancient culture, some may feel an instinctive sympathy with a people struggling for freedom, others may have the humanitarian urge to condemn the exploitation and brutal suppression of a great people by an imperialist power. But the great majority are supremely ignorant of conditions in India. They have troubles of their own; why add to them?

And yet every intelligent dabbler in public affairs knows that the problems of the modern world cannot be kept in watertight compartments; they cannot be dealt with successfully separately and without regard to the others; they run into each other and, in the final analysis, form one single world problem with many different facets. Events in the deserts and waste lands of East Africa echo in distant chancelleries and cast their heavy shadow over Europe; a shot fired in Eastern Siberia may set the world on fire. Many difficult problems trouble Europe to-day, and yet it may well be that the future historian, with a truer perspective, will consider China and India as the most significant problems of to-day, and as having a

* First published in *Vendredi* (Paris), 1936.

greater influence on the future shaping of world events. For, essentially, India and China are world problems, and to ignore them, or to minimize their significance, is to betray a woeful ignorance of the trend of world affairs and to fail to understand completely the basic disease from which all of us suffer.

The problem of India is thus of the present, of to-day. To admire or condemn her past does not help us much, except in so far as an understanding of the past helps us to understand the present. We have to realize that any big thing that will happen there will affect the larger world to a great extent, and none of us, wherever we may live and whatever national or other allegiance might claim us, can be unaffected by it. It is, therefore, from this wider point of view that we must consider it, as a part of the more immediate problems that confront us.

It is well known that the possession of India has for more than a century and a half vitally affected British foreign and domestic policy; the wealth and exploitation of India gave England the needed capital to develop her great industries in the early days of the industrial revolution and then provided her with markets for her manufactured goods; India was ever in the background in the Napoleonic wars as well as in the Crimean war; and the desire to safeguard the routes to India led England to interfere with Egypt and the countries of the Middle East. That governing policy has continued in the post-war world, and England still clings tenaciously to these routes. Soon after the Great War there even came a grandiose vision to

British statesmen of founding a great Middle Eastern Empire stretching from Constantinople to India. But that vision faded chiefly because of Soviet Russia and Kemal Pasha, and the rise of Riza Shah in Persia, and Amanullah in Afghanistan, and the establishment of the French mandate in Syria. The great idea did not materialize, but, even so, England managed to keep a fair measure of control over the land route to India and, because of this, came into conflict with Turkey over Mosul. It is that governing policy which has induced England suddenly to become a champion of the League of Nations in Ethiopia. Her moral instincts were not so much roused when the League was flouted in Manchuria.

The world problem is ultimately one of imperialism —the finance-imperialism of the present day. In Europe and elsewhere the rise of Fascism is one very important aspect of the problem, as well as the rise and growing strength of Soviet Russia, as representing a new order fundamentally opposed to that of imperialism. The lining-up of Europe in mutually hostile and anti-Fascist groups represents the conflict of that imperialism with the new forces that threaten it. In the colonial and subject countries the same conflict takes the shape of nationalist movements struggling for freedom, with an ever-developing social issue colouring and influencing nationalism. Imperialism functions increasingly in a Fascist way in its colonial dependencies. Thus England, proudly laying stress on its democratic constitution at home, acts after the Fascist fashion in India.

It is clear that any breach in the imperialist front anywhere has its repercussions all over the world. A victory of Fascism in Europe or elsewhere strengthens imperialism and reacts everywhere, a setback to it weakens imperialism. Similarly, the triumph of a freedom movement in a colonial or subject country is a blow to imperialism and Fascism, and it is therefore easy to understand why the Nazi leaders frown on Indian nationalism, and express their approval of the continuation of British domination in India. The problem, considered in its basic aspects, is simple enough, and yet, in the intricate play of various world forces, it sometimes becomes very complicated, as when two imperialisms confront one another and each tries to exploit the nationalist or anti-Fascist tendencies in the subject countries of the other. The only way to get over these complications is to consider the fundamental aspects and not to be led away by opportunist motives of gaining a temporary advantage. Else the temporary advantage is apt to prove a grave disadvantage and a burden later on.

India, both historically and by virtue of its importance, has been and is the classic land of modern imperialism. Any disturbance of the imperialist hold on India is bound to have far-reaching consequences in world affairs—it will make a tremendous difference to the world position of Great Britain, and it will give a great impetus to the freedom movements of other colonial countries and thus shake up other imperialisms. A free India would inevitably play a growing part in international affairs, and that part is likely to be on the side of world peace and against imperialism and its offshoots.

Some people imagine that India may develop into a free dominion of the British group of nations like Canada or Australia. This seems to be a fantastic idea. Even the existing dominions, in spite of their numerous links with Great Britain, are gradually drifting apart as their economic interests conflict. The drift is greatest in the case of Ireland, partly for historical reasons, and South Africa. There are few natural links between India and England, and there is a historical and ever-growing hostility between them. In many parts of the Empire there is racial ill-treatment and a policy of exclusion of Indians. But more important still, there is a conflict of economic interests. So long as India is controlled by the British Government this conflict is resolved in favour of Britain, but the moment India becomes a real dominion the two will pull different ways and a break would become inevitable, if the present capitalist order survives till then. There is another interesting aspect to this question. India, by virtue of her size, population, and potential wealth, is far the most important member of the British Empire. So long as the rest of the Empire exploits her, she remains on the imperial fringe. But a free India in the British group of nations would inevitably tend to become the centre of gravity of that group; Delhi might challenge London as the nerve-centre of the Empire. That position would become intolerable for England as well as the white dominions. They would prefer to have India outside their group, an independent but friendly country, rather than to be boss of their own household.

It seems likely, therefore, that there will be no real half-way house to Indian freedom. When India is strong enough, or when world events force the pace, she will emerge as a completely free country. What form that freedom will take and how far political freedom will be accompanied, or followed soon after, by social freedom and a new economic order, it is difficult to say, for this depends on so many factors. Inevitably world crises will affect her and hasten or delay that freedom and shape the social content of it. It is probable that the longer political freedom is delayed the more will the social question dominate the situation; even now it is in the forefront of Indian affairs. Economic conditions are forcing this issue forward, as well as the successful example of Soviet Russia.

When will Indian freedom come? It is dangerous to prophesy. But the world is moving rapidly and crisis succeeds crisis, and the weakening of the whole of British imperialism may be nearer than many people imagine. Within India the national movement has grown tremendously during the last sixteen years, ever since Mahatma Gandhi took its lead and inspired the millions to united effort and sacrifice. During these sixteen years it has continued without a break, though with ups and downs, and three times—in 1920–2, 1930–1, 1932–4—it has functioned through powerful movements of non-co-operation and civil disobedience which shook the fabric of British rule in India. The strength of these movements can be judged from the British reaction to them. This took the shape of fierce repression of the typical Fascist kind, with suppression of civil liberties, of Press, speech, and meeting, of confiscation of funds, lands, and buildings; of the proscription of hundreds of organizations, including schools, universities, hospitals, children's societies, social work clubs, and of course political and labour organizations; of the sending to prison of hundreds of thousands of men and women; and of barbarous beatings and ill-treatment of prisoners and others. On the other hand, an attempt was made to create divisions in the nationalist ranks by offering bribes and inducements to minority groups, and by consolidating all the feudal, reactionary, and obscurantist elements in the country behind the British Government. The outward symbol of this joining together of the reactionaries was the Round Table Conference in London, and the result of this union was the new "constitution" Act passed by the British Government, which in effect tightens the hold of British imperialism and gives greater importance to the reactionary element in the country.

Meanwhile new social forces have gathered strength in India and socialistic and Marxist ideas have spread, both in the ranks of organized labour and the National Congress. The Socialist Party forms an important minority in the National Congress and has an increasing influence. This rise of socialistic ideas has resulted in the development of certain fissiparous tendencies within the Congress, and further developments are likely to make this ideological cleavage more marked. On the whole, the Congress functions as a kind of joint front (including many groups)—a "front populaire"—against British imperialism, whilst in opposition to it is a joint front of the reactionary and feudal elements with that imperialism. The situation is comparable to the anti-Fascist and Fascist groupings in Europe. In between the two main groups are smaller groups of people who vacillate, though their sympathies are with the national movement.

The present position in India appears to be complex because the country is recovering from the exhaustion of the last civil disobedience movement, and during such periods a certain confusion is inevitable. New ideas find ready acceptance by many and frighten others. In spite of the fact that there is no civil disobedience movement functioning and conditions might be considered normal, the British Government are continuing their severe repression and suppression of civil liberties. In the name of suppressing communism, the Labour movement is harassed, many trade unions are declared illegal, labour leaders sent to prison; in the name of suppressing terrorism, political work is stopped in some parts of the country. Many important organizations, political and labour, continue to be banned. A law, which was contemptuously thrown out by the legislature, has been enacted by the Viceroy's executive authority, giving enormous powers to the executive and the police to suppress every form of civil liberty and public activity. Thousands are kept permanently in prison without trial or charge, many other thousands are sent to prison for sedition or other political offences. This is the functioning of British rule in India in normal times. This is also the measure of the strength of the freedom movement in India, as well as of the fear of the British Government of it. For the British Government lives in a continuous state of alarm, and when a Government is afraid it acts strangely and wildly.

It is clear that the British Government cannot succeed in putting an end to the freedom movement, it can only keep it down for a while when the nation is exhausted. It is also clear that the new Act has displeased and irritated all active elements in the country, and they can never submit to it willingly. There is more resentment and hostility against imperialist domination in India than at any previous time. Gandhi has for the time being retired from active politics, but he continues to be, and will continue to be, far and away the most dominant and influential figure in India, capable of moving millions, and he might return to the political field at any crucial moment. To imagine that he is a back number in Indian politics is the most futile of errors. There are conflicts of ideologies in India and a pulling in different directions, as is natural in a living movement in a great country, but there is unity in the opposition to British imperialism, except in those classes which profit by it, or are the creation of that imperialism. There can be little doubt that the not distant future will see great changes in India, and the approach to freedom.

All over the world to-day, behind the political and economic conflicts, there is a spiritual crisis, a questioning of old values and beliefs, and a search for a way out of the tangle. In India also, perhaps more so than elsewhere, there is this crisis of the spirit, for the roots of Indian culture still go down deep into the ancient soil, and though the future beckons, the past holds back. The old culture offers no solution of modern problems: the capitalist West, which shone so brightly in the nineteenth century, has lost its glamour, and seems to be inextricably involved in its own contradictions; the new civilization being built up in the Soviet countries attracts, in spite of some dark patches, and offers hope and world peace, and a prospect of ending the misery and exploitation of millions. It may be that India will resolve this crisis of the spirit by turning more and more to this new order, but, when it does so, it will be in her own way, making the structure fit in with the genius of her people.

12

A VISIT TO ENGLAND*

I WAS twelve days in London—twelve full days spent in meeting many people and groups, and much talk and argument and the answering of questions. I went with no particular object or intention, I sought nothing in particular except to meet some people I wanted to see and to renew my acquaintance with various currents of English thought. It was almost an educational visit for me, and though circumstances made me talk a great deal, I went to receive impressions more than to give them. Gradually I found myself drawn into all manner of environments and meeting people whom I had least expected to meet. I was a little surprised and pleased, for there was welcome and cordiality everywhere, even from those who disagreed with me utterly. My visit fitted in with my election to the presidentship of the Indian National Congress, and perhaps it was this that gave me an importance I would not have otherwise deserved. Perhaps to many people I became a symbol for a while of the suffering that my countrymen and countrywomen had undergone in recent years, and there was a vague desire to offer something in the nature of reparation. I was a poor enough symbol, for large numbers of others have gone through far greater ordeals; but I was present in the flesh and others were far away, and I sensed among

* First published in *The Socialist*, 1936.

many I met in England a kind of vague pricking of conscience at the doings of British authority in India.

It was very pleasant to meet with all this friendliness and interest in India and her problems, and yet it seemed to me that the interest was largely confined to special groups and individuals, and behind them lay the vast mass of intelligent as well as unintelligent British opinion which was tired and bored over the Indian question. They had had enough of it, other and much more interesting and important events were happening in the world and they wanted to forget about India, just as, psychologists tell us, our subconscious self makes us forget many an unpleasant occurrence which we would rather not remember. Some took comfort in the thought that the India Act being passed, India was out of the picture for many years to come. Others, not so sanguine, yet did not know what they could do; it was a damnably intricate and confusing problem, and it was best to ignore it.

These reactions were perhaps natural; they were not difficult to understand. It was not the intricacy of the problem that baffled, for it was simple enough in its essence, but the fact that any effective solution inevitably came up against the whole structure of British political and economic life, and the complex of ideas and long-cherished prejudices which the British people have held in regard to India. To solve the problem meant the knocking out of the bottom of that structure and the smothering of those ancient ideas and prejudices. It meant the ending of the imperialist tradition and the winding-up of the Empire. So attention was diverted to the failings, real or imaginary, of the Indian people, to the supposed fact that India was not a nation at all with all its races, castes, and languages, that it was largely illiterate, and of course to the communal problem. Much could be said about these various matters which would go to show that they were, after all, not so important as they were thought to be. But quite apart from their truth or importance, other facts stand out: the terrible poverty of India, the vast unemployment among all classes, the problems of land and industry, the continuing repression and denial of civil liberty by which the British Government seeks to convince us that we are being given a large dose of self-government. These problems cannot be tackled by protecting the very interests that create them and flourish on them.

The Conservative reaction was simple enough, and its very simplicity gave it an air of romance. They had few doubts or difficulties, no complexes over India. For an Indian it was a little difficult to discuss this question with them, in spite of their amiability, for we started from entirely different premises and looked different ways. We could find no common ground to stand on, no agreement to form the basis of argument. The British Empire was good, very good and beneficial to all concerned, and bound to endure. Unhappily it was surrounded by evil elements, full of spite and jealousy, who created difficulties in the smooth working of this ideal institution. If these objectionable elements could be made to see straight or be suppressed, all would be well. Some of the left-wing Conservatives were a little troubled at the close association of their party with all the reactionary and feudal elements in India; they even thought that some economic changes were necessary. But, on the whole, these ideas did not affect the essential serenity of their outlook.

Those who might be called Liberals did not differ greatly, but they were troubled more at what was happening in India, and vague fears of the future prevented them from enjoying the calm of peaceful contemplation which might otherwise have been theirs. Bred up in the traditions of civil liberty and democracy, they felt a little uneasy at the ruthless suppression in India of much they had in England. But only a little. For India was different and far away, and it was possible to still the qualms of conscience and principle by the consoling thought that, but for the repression, India might go to pieces and be converted into a sea of blood. As for democracy, were there not substantial beginnings of it in the India Act with its wider franchise, and safeguards and special powers have a way of falling into desuetude under democratic institutions? So all was well, and it was possible, with a certain measure of equanimity, to accept the present position in India, and at the same time to condemn wholeheartedly the dictatorships and suppression of freedom in Germany, Russia, Italy, the Balkans, and elsewhere.

More interesting because they were more complicated were the reactions of the Labour groups. They varied of course greatly from the Communist, looking forward to social revolution, to the Trade Union leader, vaguely wishing well to India and everybody but moving in a narrow sphere of wages and hours of work and the building up of an organization which might gain a majority in Parliament and lead to a Labour Government. It was not clear what would happen when this desirable result was achieved.

There were many individuals in the Labour movement, as well as groups, who had pinned their faith on Socialism and who were prepared to apply these principles to India. They realized that imperialism was a barrier to all real progress both in India and England, and in the ultimate interests of both this must go. It was easy for me to discuss our mutual problems with them with this basis of agreement. But for the Labour Party as a whole there was no such realization, and even when an uncomfortable feeling came that some such fundamental change was inevitable, it was sternly suppressed, and as practical men and women they faced the problem of the next Labour Government. With all their dislike for it they moved in the orbit of imperialism, and felt powerless to step out of it. Events might of course force their hands, but the initiative was not likely to come from them. They were unhappy about the past record of their party in regard to India and they wanted to make amends, but within that circle of Empire that encompassed them there was not much room for movement. And there was always the fear that any stepping out of that circle might endanger their electoral prospects and lessen their reputation for practical and respectable statesmanship.

The Labour Party has moved to the right in recent

years; the drift is likely to continue. Even in earlier days its record in India was indistinguishable from that of other parties and governments, and it gathered to itself the deep distrust of the Indian people. It will not be easy to remove this and, even with all the goodwill that many of its members undoubtedly possess for India, it can hardly do much to regain the confidence of the Indian people, unless it moves out of the circle that closes round it and makes it afraid of its own professions. A Labour Government may come back some time in the future, and much is likely to happen in India before then. Even when it comes, it will be nervous and lacking confidence in itself; it will be afraid of all manner of vested interests, and the House of Lords will be there to see that it behaves. Only international catastrophes and major events in India or elsewhere will shake it out of its lethargy.

Very interesting were many non-party men whom I met, sensitive men who though not wedded to any well-defined political policy were keenly aware of the world's disorder and of approaching catastrophe, and anxious to do their best to avert it. India was a secondary question in their minds and they were absorbed by dangers of war and the crisis of modern civilization. Mostly their approach was psychological and humanitarian, and I felt drawn towards it. And yet I felt there was something lacking in it; it was vague and idealistic without much reference to hard and cruel reality, and it did not promise any definite results. Nevertheless a widespread realization of the folly and evil in the present-day world and an ardent desire to end them was in itself a significant and hopeful sign.

The problem of India is an essential part of the world crisis, for India is the classic and most important symbol of modern imperialism. Within the fabric of imperialism there can be no solution of that crisis; it will have to go, root and branch, and the sooner this is realized and worked for, the nearer we shall all be to a solution of the world's difficulties. That seems to me the only way, and it is the way of Socialism. With that realization will come mutual confidence and co-operation between the progressive elements of India and England. Such problems as remain—and there will be many, for the period of transition is always full of difficulty—can then be faced and solved with mutual consideration and with a view to healing the world's ills. Otherwise there can only be continuous conflict and friction, with occasional eruptions bringing suffering and misery to large numbers.

Perhaps conflict is inevitable and we cannot escape it. Under present conditions it cannot be avoided, for the policy the British Government has pursued in India is a continuous invitation to conflict. But even if conflict continues, cannot it be made a little more civilized than what we have had in the past? Is it not possible to end or tone down at least the Fascist methods of brutal suppression of a sensitive people struggling for their freedom, which the British Government has been pursuing interminably for years past?

Whatever the future may hold, I shall carry back

with me to India the knowledge that there is a fund of goodwill in England for the Indian struggle, and we have many true comrades here who stand for the same Socialist ideal as many of us do and we can work together for a common cause.

13

THE WAY TO PEACE*

IN a recent speech in the House of Commons, Mr. Lloyd George pleaded for the "Have-nots" amongst the great imperialist Powers—"Have-nots" in the sense that they do not possess colonies to supply them with raw materials and provide sheltered markets for their manufactured goods. From a strictly imperialist point of view, perhaps there was some force in his argument; bribery on a big enough scale might lessen the war-hunger of these "Have-not" Powers for a while and relieve the immediate tension in Europe. It might also of course whet the appetite and increase the demand and convince the peoples and the Governments concerned that threat of and preparation for war pays. Whatever the immediate result might be, the ultimate result could hardly be doubted—the increase in rivalry between these Powers and inevitable conflicts. That has been the history of the growth of modern imperialism, and as fresh colonial areas have come under its domination, these conflicts have increased. The fact that science can provide food and leisure and an ever-increasing standard for all does not, under the peculiar system we live in, lessen these conflicts but only creates more unemployment and international friction.

As I listened to Mr. Lloyd George, it struck me as

* First published in *Time and Tide*, 1936.

very odd that he should feel so keenly for the unhappy state of the "Have-not" Powers and yet ignore completely the colonial countries and their peoples. Have they no rights in the matter or no say in it? But even apart from the rights and the moralities, is it imagined that peace will be ensured and entrenched by a sharing of the booty by the imperialist Powers?

So long as there are "haves" and "have-nots" friction and conflict will continue, and it is desirable to put an end to this state of affairs. But it seems a mockery to call powerful nations "Have-nots" and ignore the real "Have-not" countries and classes which are being dominated over and exploited. If Mr. Lloyd George's argument is to be carried to its logical conclusion, the first thing to be done is to equalize from below upwards, put an end to the exploitation of one country or people or class by another, and thus remove the causes of conflict. But that of course would mean an ending of capitalist-imperialism.

Many pacifists and others who desire ardently to prevent war imagine that the way to bring this about is by satisfying the greed of certain European nations and generally preaching goodwill to all, but otherwise maintaining the *status quo*. It does not seem to be realized by them that it is this very *status quo* that produces ill will and conflict, and is bound to lead to war. Africa may still be a helpless victim of aggression, but it is not likely to remain so for ever. India and China and several other colonial and semi-colonial countries are even now not so weak and helpless, in spite of their present condition. They can never tolerate willingly their subjection and exploitation, and they will struggle against it with all their strength. So also, as we see all around us, the classes that are exploited for the benefit of the upper strata. The *status quo* has to go throughout the world before war goes and the causes of war.

Ultimately of course this involves something more than a political or even social change; it involves a change in our habits and beliefs and instincts, and that is a terribly difficult process. But even this change in our beliefs and instincts is not likely to come till a suitable environment for it has been created.

How are these vital changes to be brought about? Gerald Heard tells us that the approach must be psychological; we must convince people that it is to their interest to have the change, we must hold a world conference in order to lay the foundations of the new era of peace and plenty. Few people will deny the importance of the psychological approach and the attempt to convert others. Facts are with us, science, reason, decency, the "spirit of the Age," enlightened self-interest, all help us. And in no event can we get a move on unless we have converted a sufficient number of people.

Granting all that, an insuperable barrier remains. It is perfectly true that the world would be a much better place to live in for all of us if we could change it to fit in with the latest developments of science and provide full scope for growth to all countries and individuals. But it is equally true that certain groups and classes which dominate to-day will lose that privileged position and, especially, the period of transition will be hard for them. They will not be convinced of the beauty of the new order or willing to accept the change. It is possible to convert individuals and even induce them to put up with loss and suffering for a larger cause, but such a conversion is not known to take place in groups and classes as a whole. They move in their own rigid ideologies and refuse to open their minds to anything which injures their group interests. Being in the seats of power they use that advantageous position to influence mass opinion in their own favour in a variety of ways and the psychological approach is thwarted by them and often neutralized.

It is hard enough to get over this difficulty in approaching even others than the groups whose self-interest is affected. But what of these groups themselves? Are we to wait indefinitely till each group and each individual concerned is converted to our ideals and objectives? And are we likely to succeed in this endeavour even after a long lapse of time? Meanwhile danger grows, and the crisis might overwhelm us while we wait and pray.

To take an instance. Must we in India convert the class or order of Indian Princes to democracy and Socialism before we can set our house in order? Granting (though it is a difficult supposition) that some individuals among them might be so converted, it is an inconceivable notion that the group will agree to give up its feudal, autocratic position. To-day most of them treat their States as their private domains where they can do what they will and can draw upon the entire State revenue for their private needs and pleasures. They will inevitably have to give all this up in any new order and they will never accept the change willingly.

Similar considerations apply to imperialist Powers and their subject countries. There is much significance in the fact that the British Government is to-day the stoutest upholder of undiluted autocracy in the Indian States, and has allied itself to all the most reactionary and obscurantist elements in India.

The psychological approach, though admirable and worth stressing, does not thus seem to be quite enough. Something more is necessary to induce the recalcitrant groups to accept or submit to the change. That something is pressure or some kind of coercion, and the bringing about of circumstances which make it more worth while for the vested interests to accept change than to suffer greater loss in an attempt to avoid it.

The application of coercion immediately conflicts with the psychological approach. We are back again where we were. Is there no way out? Cannot that coercion be applied in such a way as to minimize the fear and hatred and greed which accompany conflict and neutralize even the results of victory? Is it possible to have that psychological approach and yet have the coercion?

That, I take it, is the real problem. Pacifists, as a rule, seem to avoid it and move in an ineffective sphere. Inevitably they become upholders of an unjust system and support the very causes that lead to war. An ardent apostle of peace, a champion of sanctions against Italy, who has received the Nobel Peace Prize, tells us in India that we are narrow-minded and perverted because we do not see the beauty of the British Empire and seek to walk out of it.

I write under a certain disadvantage because I have not seen all the articles which Gerald Heard has written on this subject, and do not know what his immediate practical steps are. So far, I have failed to discover any such practical or effective steps in the proposals of the pacifists. I can hardly imagine that the proposal to hold a world peace conference will, under present conditions, lead to anything.

The only practical solution of the problem came from Gandhi. Whether that was a final solution or not remains to be seen, but it did combine the Sermon on the Mount with effective action. In considering his methods one should not be diverted by a discussion of his views on science, or modern industry, or asceticism, or birth control. The technique and the method of approach stand quite apart from those particular views though they might sometimes be coloured by them. That approach is the psychological approach, the refusal to subordinate means to an end, the constant endeavour to lessen ill will and fear, the continuous willingness to make friends of his opponents, and yet at the same time effective and dynamic action. For it must be remembered that in spite of the abundance of "nons" in his movement (non-violence, non-cooperation, etc.), it was not a negative, passive affair. It was an active, dynamic, energizing drive which lifted a whole nation out of a morass of demoralization and helplessness, the inevitable result of a long period of subjection, and removed partially at least the inferiority complex from which it suffered, and did all this with the least amount of ill will against the opposite party. Of course there were lapses and bitterness and hatred, but the surprising thing is that they were so few and that within a short term of years he could have worked this astounding change.

The effect on the Indian people was very marked, and that in itself was success enough. Equally interesting, though very different, was the effect on the British people. Individuals apart, this reaction was one of increasing hostility. Partly this was due to the suppression and distortion of Indian news in England. Fleet Street declared a ban on India, except when the antics of a maharaja were prominently figured. While millions in India were living through a nightmare of horror, most people in England no doubt imagined that all was well in this bright jewel of the British crown. But news did occasionally trickle through and, in any event, informed people always had a fair notion of what was happening. Even so, these informed and intelligent people, generous and liberal in their ideas, freedom-loving when remote people and other interests were concerned, became more and more hostile to India and her people and tolerated conditions there, of their own Government's making, which shocked them nearer home. It was a very striking example of one's own interests perverting one's sense of values and suppressing the moral sense.

In India the same reaction took place among British officials. But they were in the thick of events and could not ignore them or pass academical judgments. So they went from one brutality to another, progressively deteriorated, and what had been an abnormality, hesitatingly indulged in, became a normal daily occurrence.

Thus we see that the psychological approach did not have a very marked effect on the opposite party. It was smothered by those in power and places of authority and not allowed to reach wider groups, and even when it did so reach, the real or imaginary interests of the group prevented it from producing its expected result. Indeed the idea that the group was being placed morally in the wrong produced the strongest irritation and anger and led to the conviction that there must be something deep and diabolical about this seemingly moral approach.

Perhaps it is too soon to judge. But meanwhile all over the world the clouds gather and pacifists talk vaguely of goodwill and refuse to face realities. They will have to do something more if they wish to be effective.

14

INDIAN PROBLEMS*

MR. CARL HEATH, the Chairman, put the following questions to Mr. Nehru:

(1) Will you outline what is meant by the term "Complete Independence for India"?

(2) Do you recognize the need for an intermediate period of transition, and, if so, does the India Act in any way meet this? If not, what are the next steps to be taken?

(3) What is the relation of the Indian problem in regard to world problems? Does the League of Nations help in this connection?

(4) How far is the communal problem due to economic causes?

(5) What alternative method would you use for dealing with the situation on the North-West Frontier? And similarly for the situation in Bengal?

(6) In what ways can people in this country help? What part do you think a Conciliation Group can play?

(7) Should not the Indian National Movement maintain some kind of effective agency in

* Record of a meeting held in London, February 4, 1936, under the auspices of the Indian Conciliation Group.

London for the purpose of spreading accurate information?

Mr. Jawaharlal Nehru: Mr. Chairman and friends, first of all may I point out that, although I happen to have been elected the President of the next session of the Indian National Congress, I do not speak in any such capacity but entirely on my own behalf. In any event I should not have been able to speak as President of the Congress, but that is especially so because I have been really cut off from my colleagues and the leaders of the Congress movement in India for a number of years, and it is difficult for me to get into touch with living currents of thought in India without being in that country for some time.

These questions that have been framed are fairly comprehensive. One could say a great deal about them or deal with them briefly. I suppose it would be best if I tried to deal with them fairly briefly, because there is not very much time at our disposal this afternoon, and I shall try (although I am not likely to succeed) to say only that which is pertinent to the subjects dealt with in the questions.

(1) With regard to the first question: "Will you outline what is meant by the term 'Complete independence for India'?" presumably the reference is to this phrase occurring in the first Article of the Congress Constitution. Therein it refers, I take it, to the political side only and not to the economic side. Of course, the Congress as a whole is beginning to think on economic lines also and otherwise develop its economic policy,

and some of us, including myself, think much more on the lines of economic freedom than on the lines of political freedom. Obviously economic freedom includes political freedom. But, defining this phrase simply in its political sense, as it occurs in the Congress Constitution, it means national freedom, not only domestic but foreign, financial, military, i.e. control of the military and control of foreign affairs; in other words, whatever national freedom usually signifies. That does not mean necessarily that we lay stress on an isolation of India or a breaking away of India from such associations as might exist with England or with other countries, but it does mean—the word "independence" is used specially to lay stress on the fact—that we want to break the imperialist connection with Britain. If imperialism survives in England, we must part from England, because, so long as imperialism survives in England, the only connection between England and India is likely to be the connection of an imperialist domination in India in some form or other. It may become vaguer and vaguer; it may become less obvious than it is; it may even not be obvious on the political side and yet be very powerful on the economic side. Therefore in terms of imperialist Britain the independence of India means the separation of India from England. Personally I can conceive and welcome the idea of a close association between India and England on terms other than those of imperialism.

(2) The second question is: "Do you recognize the need for an intermediate period of transition, and, if

so, does the India Act in any way meet this? If not, what are the next steps to be taken?" Whenever any change comes about, inevitably there are all manner of intermediate and transitional phases, but often it so happens that the structure of government becomes rather petrified and does not change rapidly enough, while economic and other changes are inevitably going on, because economic changes do not wait for laws and enactments; they go on while the structure does not change. The result is that in extreme cases there are big upheavals which forcibly change the structure, and those are called revolutions, but even in that case there are transition periods. I take it that this question refers more to the structure of government than to any intermediate period and it is therefore difficult to answer, because that depends on so many factors. It depends partly on us but largely on the British Government and largely on various forces, national and international. Obviously if there was a mutual arrangement between Britain and the people of India there would inevitably be transitional stages in the process of reaching that goal. It might take a long time, but there would have to be some steps in the process; one cannot suddenly and all at once bring about a big change. On the other hand, if there is no possibility of a change being brought about by mutual agreement, then there are likely to be upheavals, and it is difficult to say what the result of an upheaval will be. It depends on the size of the upheaval; it depends on the great economic forces that cause the upheaval, and anything might happen, because, as I conceive it, the fundamental problem of India really is economic in its various aspects. The chief problem is the land problem, with its enormous amount of unemployment and over-pressure on land, and connected with that is the industrial problem, because probably if one tries to solve the land problem one will have to consider the question of industry. There are also many other problems, such as unemployment in the middle classes, and they will really have to be tackled all together, so that they may fit into each other, and not individually and separately.

All these problems have to be tackled for many reasons, but the fundamental reason is that the economic situation is growing worse and the condition of the vast masses is going further and further down. They cannot be tackled by merely changing the political structure at the top. The political structure might be such as to help us in tackling the problems, and the real test of the political structure is this: Does it help us and will it make it easier for us to tackle these problems and solve them?

With regard to an intermediate period, therefore, all one can say is that there is bound to be some intermediate period. We are passing through an intermediate period now, but whether the development is going to be by arrangement or agreement or by sudden jumps or big jumps the future alone can show.

In India the Congress and some groups outside the Congress have suggested that the proper and democratic way to deal with the political aspect of the problem is by means of a Constituent Assembly, that is to say, fundamentally the people of India should decide the Constitution of India; they do not admit that the people of India should remain merely passive agents of a foreign authority in regard to the drawing up of such a Constitution. The only way in which the desires of the people of India can take shape is through some such Constituent Assembly. To-day that is not a feasible proposition, simply because it cannot be put into effect unless the British Government itself decides to put an end to its domination in India and leave the Indian people to develop their own Constitution, or, whether the British Government so decides or not, the pressure of events brings it about, because a real Constituent Assembly involves ultimately or, in fact, in the near future after it is formed, the end of British domination in India. A Constituent Assembly does not mean merely a group of so-called leaders coming together and drawing up a Constitution. The whole idea behind the Constituent Assembly is this: that it should be elected by means of an adult franchise, men and women together, so that there should be really mass representation, in order to give effect to the economic urges of the masses. The present difficulty is that a number of upper middle-class people sit down and, instead of talking in terms of economics, they discuss the question of offices in the new Constitution and who will be appointed to them; there is a desire to share in the spoils of office, in patronage, and so forth, which the new Constitution might bring, and that partly gives rise to the communal problem. If the mass elements take part in the election of the Constituent Assembly, obviously they will not be interested in getting jobs in the new Constitution; they are interested in their own economic troubles and attention will immediately be given to social and economic issues, whilst some of the other problems, which appear to loom large but are fundamentally not important, will recede into the background, like the communal problem.

The second part of the question is: Does the India Act in any way meet the need for an intermediate period of transition? I have just said that the test of a Constitution is this: Whether it helps us to solve the economic problems which face us and which are the real problems. The India Act, as you perhaps know, has been criticized from almost every possible angle by almost every possible group in India, moderate or advanced. I doubt if it has any friends at all in India. If there are a few persons who are prepared to tolerate it, either they belong to the big vested interests in India or they are people who by sheer habit tolerate everything that the British Government does. Apart from those people, almost every political group in India has taken the strongest exception to the India Act. They all object to it and have criticized it in very great detail, and the general feeling is that, far from helping us, it really takes us back and it binds our hands and feet so tightly that we cannot get a move on. All the vested interests in Britain and in India have found such a permanent place in this Act that any substantial social or economic change or political change becomes almost impossible, short of revolution. On the one hand, under the India Act we cannot even endeavour to make substantial economic changes; on the other hand, we cannot change the India Act itself. You must not think that in the India Act we are getting some democratic instrument which can be developed into something better. That is not so. You must not apply the analogy of the various steps taken in the Dominions—in Canada and in Australia —in the early stages of the development of self-government in those countries. The problems there were very simple; there were simple communities to be dealt with, and, whatever the steps taken were, there was room for inevitable development, and that development did take place. That does not apply to India at all. To-day India has not to face a simple problem; it has to face a very complicated economic problem and the decision to be taken on that problem cannot be postponed. Secondly, the India Act is such that it cannot be developed. Of course, there can be development from time to time if the British Government itself changes the India Act, but, as it is, even if 99 or 100 per cent of the people of India want to change it they cannot do so. It has no seeds of change in it; it is a permanent fixing of the chains of vested interest on the Indian people. The only choice that is offered to the Indian people is to submit to it or, if they want to change it, to revolt against it in some form or other. Therefore the India Act does not in any way meet the need for an intermediate period of transition. Under the India Act a wider electorate is created, and that is a desirable thing, but it is the only desirable thing in the Act.

(3) The third question is: "What is the relation of the Indian problem in regard to the world problems? Does the League of Nations help in this connection?" I think that nearly all the major problems that we have to face in the world to-day—in Europe or India or China or America—are intimately connected together, and it is really difficult to understand any one of them or ultimately to solve any one of them without thinking of the other problems. The different parts of the world to-day are becoming extraordinarily interrelated with each other, and events which happen in one part of the world immediately react and interact upon the other parts of the world. If there is a big thing such as an international war, obviously the whole world is upset. If there is an economic crisis—we have had a very big one in the last few years—that affects the whole world. These big waves and movements affect the whole world, and obviously the Indian problem is intimately connected with other problems. Anything big that happens in India obviously affects the whole British group of nations—British imperialism. Anything that affects British imperialism makes a great difference in the world, because British imperialism to-day is a very important factor in world politics. So far as India is concerned, it is a well-known fact that India has had the greatest influence on British foreign policy in the last hundred years or so. During the Napoleonic period India loomed large; although perhaps when you read about the Napoleonic cam-

paigns you find that India is seldom mentioned, it was in the background all the time. Whether it was the Crimean War or the occupation of Egypt, always there was the question of India in the background and the routes to India. The routes to India have often been before British statesmen. Perhaps some of you may remember that even after the Great War there was an idea, fostered by Mr. Winston Churchill and some of the leading figures in British public life, of having an enormous Middle Eastern Empire from the borders of India to Constantinople, but it did not take shape. It sounds rather curious now, but at that time, after the war, all that area was in British occupation; Persia was in British occupation, and so were Mesopotamia, Palestine, parts of Arabia, and Constantinople. Therefore the idea was not such a fanciful one as it seems to be now, but various things happened to prevent it taking shape; there was the Soviet Government and there were events in Turkey and Persia, and so forth, and the whole thing was upset by various developments. Even so, the object of the British Government was to control the land route to India, because the land route was becoming important, owing to the development of aeroplanes and motor traffic. The question of Mosul nearly brought about conflict between Turkey and England, chiefly because Mosul dominates the land route to India.

Therefore from many points of view the question of India affects world problems very greatly. Anything that happens to India inevitably affects other countries.

With regard to the League of Nations in this connection, the League of Nations might perhaps help India if the Indian viewpoint was put before it properly and pressed before it, but so far the position has been that India has really nothing to do with the League of Nations except that it is represented on the League. The so-called Indian representatives on the League of Nations are nominated by the Government of India in consultation with the British Government, so that they really represent on the League the viewpoint of the British Government; they do not represent in the slightest Indian public opinion. Therefore you might say that India is not represented at all on the League of Nations, but that the British Government gets an extra representative. If India could be properly represented, I suppose the League of Nations would do some good, although fundamentally the League of Nations, of course, is an organization for the maintenance of the *status quo* in the world, and obviously the Indian people desire to change their *status quo*. Therefore, if they laid any fundamental proposition before the League of Nations, it would probably be barred under some section of the Covenant or of the rules under which the League functions, on the ground that it would interfere with the domestic policy of the British Empire.

(4) With regard to the fourth question: "How far is the communal problem due to economic causes?" this question perhaps is not properly framed (I am partly responsible for that), in the sense that the communal question is not fundamentally due to economic causes. It has an economic background which often

influences it, but it is due much more to political causes. It is not due to religious causes; I should like you to remember that. Religious hostility or antagonism has very little to do with the communal question. It has something to do with the communal question in that there is a slight background of religious hostility which has in the past sometimes given rise to conflict and sometimes to broken heads, in the case of processions and so forth, but the present communal question is not a religious one, although sometimes it exploits religious sentiment and there is trouble. It is a political question of the upper middle classes which has arisen partly because of the attempts of the British Government to weaken the national movement or to create rifts in it, and partly because of the prospect of political power coming into India and the upper classes desiring to share in the spoils of office. It is to this extent economic, that the Mohammedans, the Moslems, are on the whole the poorer community as compared with the Hindus. Sometimes you find that the creditors are the Hindus and the debtors the Mohammedans; sometimes the landlords are Hindus and the tenants are Mohammedans. Of course, the Hindus are tenants also, and they form the majority of the population. It sometimes happens that a conflict is really between a moneylender and his debtors or between a landlord and his tenants, but it is reported in the Press and it assumes importance as a communal conflict between Hindus and Mohammedans. Fundamentally this communal problem is a problem of the conflict between the members of the upper middle-class

Hindus and Moslems for jobs and power under the new Constitution. It does not affect the masses at all. Not a single communal demand has the least reference to any economic issues in India or has the least reference to the masses. If you examine the communal demands you will see that they refer only to seats in the legislature or to various kinds of jobs which might be going in the future.

(5) The next question is: "What alternative method would you use for dealing with the situation on the North-West Frontier? And similarly for the situation in Bengal?" Briefly put, the alternative method I would suggest is the method of conciliation plus some kind of effort to deal with the problem on economic lines, because fundamentally the difficulty of the frontier men is scarcity. They live in a hard country, on the mountain sides, and they come down in search of food and loot. Personally I do not think the frontier problem is very difficult of solution. If a proper and friendly approach is made, I think it ought to be solved fairly easily. As a matter of fact, my own impression is that a similar—not exactly the same, but a similar—problem was faced in the nineteenth century by the Russian Government, that is to say, the old Tsarist Government, because their frontier was fairly near and they had to deal with more or less the same type of people. So far as I know, they never had any great difficulty in dealing with them; certainly they did not have the amount of difficulty that the British Government has had for a hundred years or so. If one thing is obvious it is this, that the British Government's

frontier policy has been a dismal and total failure. If they are unable to settle the frontier question after having dealt with it for generations, having had every year, or every other year, a military expedition with slaughter and bombing and all the rest of it, obviously there is something wanting in their policy. The Tsarist Government never had to face all the difficulties which the British Government has to face, the reason being, I think, that the Tsarist Government made it possible for the frontier men to lead a more normal life; they tried to colonize them, to settle them on the land. I am only putting this forward as a suggestion; I do not know enough about the matter to state definitely why the Tsarist Government did not have the same difficulty that the British Government has in dealing with the frontier men. Anyhow, the population involved is not large, and it should not be difficult to deal with them on economic lines, so that this economic urge might disappear. For the rest, obviously the approach must be friendly and not like the recent approach of the Italians in Abyssinia. That kind of approach has failed completely. The frontier men are very brave people; they do not very much care whether they live or die, but they do not like to be dominated. They are freedom-loving people, as mountain people often are, and the British Government has not been able to subdue them permanently. It can conquer them from time to time but it cannot subdue them.

With regard to a friendly approach, for years past Mr. Gandhi has been invited by the frontier people to go to them. I believe he went to the Frontier Province some years ago, but he has never crossed the frontier or gone right up to it. His name, however, is very well known on both sides of the frontier. He is very popular with the frontier men and repeated invitations have been extended to him to visit them, but the Government has not allowed him to do so. He did not want to go in defiance of the wishes of the Government; he did not want to invite conflict on that issue, so whenever he wanted to go he always referred the matter to the Viceroy or the Government of India, saying: "I have been asked to go there and I should like to go," and he always got the same answer, to this effect: "We strongly advise you not to go." That was almost tantamount to an order, and so he has not gone. Apart from Mr. Gandhi, the great leader of the Frontier Province, Abdul Ghaffar Khan, has quite an extraordinary influence and popularity all over that region. It is astounding how he has become such a tremendous figure in that area. That in itself, of course, was quite sufficient to make the British Government dislike him intensely. A man who has such a commanding influence over these turbulent Pathans is a man who will not be liked by any Government agency. He therefore spends his time in prison; he is in prison at the present moment. After two or three years of detention without trial he came out last year, but he was out for only three months, and then he was sent back to prison for a two years' sentence, which he is serving now. As you perhaps know, he is a member of the highest Congress Executive. He is one of the most popular men not only on the frontier but in the whole of India. You will realize from his name that he is a Mohammedan and not a Hindu. He is one of the greatest Moslem leaders of the masses in India. He occupies one of the highest positions in the Congress movement. You must remember that the Congress movement, although it is inevitably composed chiefly of Hindus, has a very stiff backing of Moslems. Therefore if Abdul Ghaffar Khan and Mr. Gandhi did go to the frontier I think they would have the most magnificent reception there, and they could discuss the frontier problem there with others. I do not think it would be very difficult to solve that problem. I do not mean to say that such a visit would put an end to all troubles; that is absurd. Certain troubles will arise again and again, but the foundations of stability could be laid, and if some economic remedies were also applied I think an end could be definitely put to this recurring trouble.

With regard to Bengal, terrorism in Bengal has gained far greater prominence and advertisement than it really deserves. That it has existed there, and that it exists there now to some extent is undeniable, but, after all, when you come to think of it, if in a country like India or a great province like Bengal one or two terrorist acts are committed in the course of two or three years (in the last two years, I think, none have taken place and in the year before there were one or two), although it is deplorable it is not such a terrible thing. We must not lose our sense of proportion in this matter. That is the first fact I want to put before you. Secondly, so far as my knowledge goes (obviously

I have no direct immediate knowledge, because I have been in prison for two or three years), there is really no organized terrorist movement now. There was, but I do not think there is now in Bengal or elsewhere in India. I do not mean by that that people in Bengal or elsewhere do not believe in methods of violence; there are many who believe in methods of violence and revolution, but I think that even those who used to believe in acts of terrorism do not do so now; that is to say, the old terrorists, or many of them, still think that in all probability some kind of armed violence might be necessary to fight the dominating power, but they think in terms of insurrection, violence, or some kind of organized revolt; they do not think in terms of throwing bombs or shooting down people. Many of them, I think, were drawn completely away from the terrorist movement by Mr. Gandhi's peaceful movement, but even those who remained turned away from the purely terrorist attitude, which, as you know, is a very infantile attitude in political movements. When a national movement begins there is always a certain background of sentiment and helplessness and hopelessness which drives an excited youth to an act of terrorism, but, as the movement develops and grows stronger, the energy of the people is directed towards organized activity, towards mass action, and so forth. That has happened in India, and inevitably the terrorist movement has practically ended, but the extraordinary amount of terrible repression that has gone on in Bengal inevitably gives rise to some reprisals on the part of the old terrorist group. For instance, an individual may become exceedingly bitter because of certain things that have happened to his own friends in his own city. Terrible things are happening there, and as a reaction the individual or two or three individuals may decide on an act of reprisal directed towards the person who did those things. That has nothing to do with terrorism as an organization; it is purely an individual act of reprisal. Such an act of terrorism sometimes occurs, but, as I have said, even that has not happened for the last two years. Again, the old terrorists are more or less well known to the police. Many of them are interned or imprisoned and many of them have been executed, but a number of them, I suppose, are still about. I met one of them two or three years ago. He was a big man in the terrorist movement in the old days, and he came to see me and said: "I am definitely of opinion that these acts of terrorism are no good. I do not want to do them. I am inducing my people not to do them. But what am I to do? I am hunted like a dog. I go about from place to place. I know that whenever I am caught I shall have to suffer the death penalty. I do not propose to do that. When I am caught I shall shoot in self-defence." One often finds that it is when an old terrorist has been rounded up or is on the point of being caught that he shoots. The net closes round him, and he prefers shooting and being shot and dying in that way to being sent to the gallows.

What I mean is this: the movement is not functioning at all in an aggressive way. Sometimes an individual may commit an act of terrorism in a moment of excitement or in self-defence when he is being caught; otherwise terrorism is over. Obviously when such a thing happens it has some psychological or other roots from which it arises, and it is quite absurd to deal with it by a permanent system of martial law. The average military mind can think of a solution to a problem only in terms of martial law, and, unfortunately for us, in India the average civilian mind has been functioning largely in a military way. Obviously a terrorist plays with his own life. He may be going to lose his life at the very moment when he commits an act of terrorism. For instance, when a person goes into a crowded hall and shoots another person, obviously his or her life is forfeit. I cannot see how a person who is prepared to give up his life can be terrified by any military measures which may be taken. He knows when he carries out his terroristic enterprise that he is bound to die; usually he carries a little poison in his pocket and swallows it after the act. What happens is that a large number of innocent people suffer.

(6) The next question is: "In what ways can people in this country help? What part do you think a Conciliation Group can play?" That is not a very easy question for me to answer—though I have endeavoured to answer it in various places—because it depends on changing conditions here, but certainly a great deal can be done if people really do take an interest in the Indian problem and think that it requires, both from the point of view of India and from the point of view

of the world, a suitable solution. I do not suppose that in the present circumstances individual groups can make very much difference; that is to say, they cannot change Government policy, though they might affect it in minor matters. But I think such groups can always keep conditions in India in the forefront here. For instance, even now there is no realization amongst the British people of the quite extraordinary amount of repression and denial of civil liberties that is going on in India. I am told that about a month ago there was some reference in Parliament to political prisoners. Some Labour Members raised the question, and some Conservative Members said: "What! Are there still any political prisoners in India?" That question shows the amazing ignorance that prevails on the subject. There is a very large number of people in India who have been detained without trial for five years, six years, and various other periods, a large number of ordinary political prisoners are being convicted from day to day and the whole apparatus of repression is functioning from day to day. I think the average Englishman or Englishwoman does not require much detailed knowledge of Indian problems to understand the problem of civil liberty; the average English person does feel that civil liberty is a desirable thing, and, when the facts of the situation in India are put before him, he is somewhat shocked; he dislikes the utter denial of civil liberty in India. I think a great deal can be done by keeping all these facts before the people of this country, and much can be done in that way by co-operation between various groups. I believe there is a National Council for Civil Liberties here, and that could usefully co-operate with other groups in the direction I have indicated.

With regard to specific Indian problems, especially the economic conditions, the way in which the political problem depends on the economic problem is of importance, because when that subject is considered the political problem is viewed in its proper perspective. Otherwise you function in the air, as we have been functioning at these Round Table Conferences and other conferences. A number of lawyers sit down and produce a paper Constitution which has no relation to the existing facts or position in India but has relation to only one fact, that is, that the vested interests in India want to perpetuate their existence.

Therefore any group in this country can certainly help the cause of India, and not only the cause of India but, as I think one might say, having regard to the question of civil liberties and other matters which are involved, the cause of humanity. A group could go much further if it decided to adopt the political and economic standpoint of the advanced groups, but, however far it goes, it can, I think, function effectively.

As for the Conciliation Group, I have been told that it is not an organization but a group with no specially defined limits. Such a group, I think, has done good work in the past, and I believe it can certainly do good work in the future. I have suggested that it would be desirable for the various groups interested in India as a whole or in particular questions, such as the question of civil liberties, to keep in touch with each other. They need not merge into each other, because they have different outlooks. There is no reason why one group should adopt the outlook of another group. One may not be prepared to commit itself to some points to which another group is committed, but still they may have a great deal in common. There is no reason why they should not occasionally meet together or representatives of them confer together, so that their activities might not overlap but might supplement each other.

(7) The last question is: "Should not the Indian National Movement maintain some kind of effective agency in London for the purpose of spreading accurate information?" I think that would be a highly desirable thing, and I doubt whether anybody would object in principle to it. You must remember that during the last six years India has gone through a very abnormal period. During four years of that time the Congress has been an illegal movement. We always hover on the edge of illegality; we do not know when we might be termed illegal, our funds confiscated, our property confiscated, and our offices confiscated. That makes it a little difficult to develop a foreign agency in the ordinary way, but certainly this is desirable, and I should very much like to have some kind of information bureau here and, it may be, in some other parts of Europe, to function, apart from questions of propaganda, by giving accurate information and providing books and papers, so that people who want that information might be able to obtain it.

THE CHAIRMAN: I think we must all feel that in

dealing with these questions Mr. Nehru has given us a series of pictures of the main problems of India to-day, and he has done so in an extraordinarily interesting and lucid way. He will now answer any questions that members of the audience may like to put.

QUESTION: We sometimes meet with the objection or the criticism that if the British withdrew from India it would only open the way for Japan. It used to be Russia, but now it is Japan that is mentioned in that connection. Might we hear Mr. Nehru's opinion on that?

MR. NEHRU: It seems to me that the people who say that do not know very much about the present position or the probable future position of Japan with regard to India. The question can be considered in many ways, but I would put it to you briefly thus: How do you expect Japan to come to India, by sea or by land? Do you expect Japan to come to India after having subjugated the whole of China or before it has done so?

You must realize that it takes a little longer to go from India to Japan than it takes to go from India to England by sea. By the land route, by air, it takes a very little time to go from England to India, but it takes a very long time to go to Japan. One cannot go easily over the Himalaya Mountains and the various deserts and other tracts of China. Therefore you must realize that India is not very easily accessible to Japan if Japan goes through China, so Japan has to come by a fairly intricate route through the Singapore

Straits, and any hostile fleet could make it difficult for the Japanese to approach India. Even so, of course, Japan might come, but the real point is this, that Japan can never think in terms of the conquest of India so long as it has not completely subjugated China and made it part of its Empire. The conquest of China is a very difficult matter. At the moment Japan has overrun North China and it may perhaps extend further south, but I do not think that anyone acquainted with the history of China or the present position of China or the international position, imagines that Japan is likely to succeed in consolidating her Empire in the whole of China. China is a tremendous problem for Japan, and, even if it is conquered, it will continue to be a problem and something which will really absorb the energies of Japan, and probably bring about its downfall. Look at Japan as it stands to-day as a World Power. It seems very strong. Nobody interferes with Japan's territorial instincts and activities. It does what it likes in North China and Manchuria. Yet fundamentally the position of Japan in the world is a very unhappy position. It is isolated from the rest of the world; it has no friends in the world. On the one side there is a tremendous Power, America, and there is not much love lost between Japan and the United States of America. On the other side there is China, which, although weak in one sense, is very strong in many ways. It is strong fundamentally, because its passive strength is great; its inertia is terrible. But, even apart from that, the weakness of China to-day in the face of aggression is very largely due, I think, to the fact that some of the Chinese leaders are false to China; they are betraying China. It is not so much the weakness of China as the weakness of her leaders, Chiang Kai-shek and others, and this may lead to the overthrow of Chiang Kai-shek and some kind of a combined and powerful resistance later on. Therefore, in any event, Japan would have a hostile China to deal with, whether it was subjugated or not. With America on one side and China on the other, and the Soviet Republic in the north, which is always likely to be hostile, that Japan should embark on an adventure in India, three weeks' journey away, is to me inconceivable. Then, of course, India presumably would not sit idle. It may not be a strong country, but obviously it would do its utmost to defend itself against any aggression.

QUESTION: We do not want to talk about only this aspect of the question, but I should like to say that Mr. Nehru seemed to me, in talking about this, to refer only to the internal aspect of the North-West Frontier question. Surely it has an external aspect also, and has had such an aspect for the last hundred years. We need not go so far as China and Japan and the Far East to consider that, because even in the very latest pronouncements of the Government of India reference is made to the danger—a very immediate and close danger—of Russian aggression. There we come up against that imperialistic policy which has dominated the whole of the history of the North-West Frontier, and that imperialism which Mr. Nehru says must be got rid of before he can come to any terms at all with Great Britain. What will be the position on the North-West Frontier if that imperialism is really discarded? What will be the position as regards the security of India if that imperialism, which means constant jealousy and fear and suspicion between the two great Powers, Soviet Russia and Great Britain, is finally abolished? What will be the position with regard to the defence policy of India, and what will then be the result in the organization and the cost of the Indian army?

MR. NEHRU: The result of the allaying of that suspicion would be peace and contentment on the frontier. With regard to the defence of India against Soviet aggression——

QUESTIONER: And Afghanistan; that is also an element.

MR. NEHRU: Yes, an element. Afghanistan is an unadvanced, industrially backward country, and as an effective military force it is strong only within its own territories. It is a difficult country to invade, because it is a mountainous country and the people are good fighters, but as an invading country it has no strength at all, so we can leave Afghanistan out of consideration.

With regard to Soviet Russia, the first proposition is that there is no Power in the world to-day which is more peaceful and less inclined to aggression than Soviet Russia. I think that is admitted by everybody; it is publicly admitted by the British Foreign Office; in fact, the Foreign Secretary, Mr. Eden, said so the other day.

QUESTIONER: The Government of India does not say that; it says the exact opposite.

MR. NEHRU: For various reasons. You can examine that. Soviet Russia from an economic point of view does not require India in the least, as Japan might, because India is a source of raw materials for England. Raw materials exist in sufficient quantities in Soviet territories. In minor matters India might help. Fundamentally Soviet Russia does not require India; it has not that economic urge. At the present moment it is absolutely full of its own economic problems of development, and it wants to take no risk at all of war or adventure. Obviously an invasion of India is a very big risk, not so much because of the strength of India but because any such thing involves to-day international complications, whether the invader is Japan or Russia. If Japan comes to India it is not a question merely of defeating the people of India, but there is the risk of having to fight on various fronts. Other Powers step in, and international complications are introduced. So that Russian policy to-day (nobody can say what will happen thirty years hence) is bound to be an extraordinarily peaceful policy; there is no doubt about that. If it were not, Russia would immediately be afraid of trouble from Japan in the East and from Germany in the West. We know that many European countries fear Russia to-day. The biggest factor at work is a great fear complex of being attacked, and so the countries go on increasing their military machines. So that there is no question of expecting, in the ordinary course, an invasion from Russia. So far as I am personally concerned, I very largely approve of the Russian system of government, and I hope some such thing will extend to India. I think we ought to be the most friendly of neighbours instead of being in conflict with each other. But, apart from that, obviously India, whatever its system of government is, whether Socialist or not, will have to take steps to guard her frontiers.

QUESTIONER: Against whom?

MR. NEHRU: It does not matter. The steps taken may not be very extensive, but India will have to take some steps. If the world continues to be divided up into various capitalist States, armies will have to be kept. It is relatively easy, I think, to protect India on the north-west frontier. You have probably read histories of various invasions of India from the north-west, but those histories exaggerate a little. There have been invasions, but if you spread them out over a period of two or three thousand years they have not been so frequent as some people seem to think. Those invasions took place not because of the strength of the attacking force but because at the time there was internal trouble in India, and the attacking force simply walked in. An attacking force can always be stopped on the north-west frontier by an efficient army without any great numbers being employed. An efficient defence force must be built up to defend India from invasion; one has to face the risk of these things. One of the countries suffering most from a terrible fear of invasion is also at the same time one of the most powerful countries in the military sense, that is, France. France is terribly afraid of a Nazi invasion, and yet it has one of the biggest military machines in the world.

QUESTION: The question has not actually arisen in the course of Mr. Nehru's addresses, but it might be of interest to know what his view is with regard to the contributions that may be expected from Indian women in the regeneration of India.

MR. NEHRU: Those contributions have been considerable. Indian women in the last fifteen or sixteen years have played a tremendous part in our national movement. You may remember that in 1930 Mr. Gandhi started the civil disobedience movement in connection with the Salt Tax, and I think the most important and significant feature of that movement was the tremendous part that the women of India took in it. It was astonishing. Most of us were astounded by what we saw. It was not as if we had to push them out; they simply came out and took charge of the situation when most of their menfolk were in prison, and they functioned in an extraordinarily efficient way. The surprising thing was that, although many of them had had no experience of public activity, yet they became good organizers and they ran the whole movement practically without any men for a long time. They ran it not only very well but in a much more uncompromising way than the men might have done; they did become much more uncompromising about it in every way. That was such an eye-opener that I do not think after that any person in India dares to say that the women of India are going to play a subordinate part in the public life of India in the future. Of course, as you know, they have suffered in the past and they still suffer from a large number of social and semi-religious disabilities They are trying to remove them, and to some extent they have to fight the inevitable reactions of men in that process. Certain orthodox elements in the community are trying to prevent them from removing these disabilities, but I think they are sufficiently alive to their task, and I do not think anyone can really stop them from carrying it out. So far as the national movement is concerned, the mere fact that such large numbers of women have taken such a large part in it makes it absolutely impossible for any nationalist to conceive of keeping them down in any political or social sense. The Fundamental Rights Resolution which the Congress passed some years ago laid down as a fundamental right in the Constitution the removal of all disabilities and the absolute equality of women with men in the eyes of the Constitution.

QUESTION: In your answer to the fourth question, regarding the communal problem, you suggested, I think, that the religious element was a small part of it and that it was not primarily economic, but that it resolved itself into political jealousy, political ambitions. How do you see it resolving in the light of the national movement? Do you feel that the central national aim would be so big that it would bring all the parties together?

MR. NEHRU: No. First of all I said that the communal movement was not religious, but that does not mean, of course, that there is not a religious background in India, and sometimes that is exploited. It is political mainly. It is also economic in the sense that the political problem largely arises because of the problem of unemployment in the middle classes, and it is the unemployment among the middle classes that helps the communal movement to gain importance. It is there that the jobs come in. To some extent the growth of nationalism and the nationalist spirit suppresses the communal idea, but fundamentally it will go when economic issues and social issues come to the forefront and divert the attention of the masses, and even of the lower middle classes, because these issues really affect them, and inevitably then the communal leaders would have to sink into the background. That happened in 1921, at the time of the first non-co-operation movement, when no communal leaders in India dared to come out into the open. There was no meeting held and there was no reference to them in the papers. They disappeared absolutely because there was such a big movement on other issues. As soon as a big political movement starts the communal leaders come to the forefront. They are always being pushed to the front by the British Government in India. Therefore the right way to deal with the communal question is to allow economic questions affecting the masses to be discussed. One of the chief objections to the India Act is that, because it divides India into seven or eight—I am not sure how many—separate religious compartments, it makes it difficult for economic and social questions to be brought up. Of course they will come up, because there is the economic urge behind them, but still it makes it difficult.

QUESTION: Do not you think caste comes into the communal question at all—Brahman against non-Brahman? That is a matter we know so well in Madras.

MR. NEHRU: I do not think the communal question is affected much by caste. In South India, of course, the question of caste comes in, and it has given rise to great bitterness. I was thinking more of Hindu *versus* Moslem. I am not personally acquainted with conditions in the South in recent years, but it used to be more a question of non-Brahman *versus* the vested interest. Taking the depressed classes, they really are the proletariat in the economic sense; the others are the better-off people. All these matters can be converted into economic terms, and then one can understand the position better. I do not think the Brahman and the non-Brahman question as such is very important now. There is a very large number of non-Brahmans in the Congress. In the Congress the question does not arise. It has some importance in local areas in the South, because of various local factors, but I do not think the question of Brahman and non-Brahman comes into the communal question at all.

QUESTION: Referring to the present Government of India Act and the possibility of it becoming a transition to something that India would desire, Mr. Nehru suggested that there were certain economic aims that India had which could not possibly be given any expression under the present Act and would lead to clashes. Could Mr. Nehru tell us what, in his opinion, is the way that India should develop in regard to economic arrangements and systems?

MR. NEHRU: Whatever I say on this subject will be my own personal view, because I cannot say that India as a whole desires what I desire.

Fundamentally we have to face the land problem chiefly, and the problem of unemployment, which is connected with it. I think that nothing short of large-scale collectivist or co-operative farming will deal effectively with the land question. These wretched small holdings will then disappear. Production will greatly increase and many other benefits will follow, but unemployment would not be affected thereby. In fact, by scientific farming it is possible that unemployment might even increase a little, as far as direct employment on the land is concerned, though indirectly other avenues of employment would be opened up. In order to provide employment we must absorb people in industrial development, in cottage industries, in big machine industries, and in the enormous development of the social services, such as education, hygiene, and sanitation. There are practically no social services in India to-day. The development of industry and the land would have to be planned as a whole; it cannot be dealt with in sections. If one tries to tackle one part, one finds something left over which one cannot provide for. The whole basis should be, in my opinion, not the profit motive, but producing for consumption, because if we produce for profit the result is that we simply glut the markets; we cannot sell the goods, because people have no money with which to buy them, and so we get over-production while at the same time many people have nothing at all. We should organize on the Socialist basis and have large-scale agriculture, co-operative or collectivist, big machine industries and cottage industries. The cottage industries must not be such as would be likely to conflict with big industries, because then they would collapse, but I think there will be plenty of room for the growth of cottage industries for a long time to come, simultaneously with the growth of big industries. If big industries are not developed on a capitalist basis, they will deal with the essentials which are required and there will be no needless waste of energy. If all these things are taken together, I imagine we might go a little way towards the solution of the various problems that confront us. I cannot see any movement in that direction under present conditions.

Questioner: You mean something similar to the Soviet system of the organization of industry and agriculture?

Mr. Nehru: I personally should like to have something similar to that, but I was really envisaging something much less for the moment. I do not want India to be drilled and forced into a certain position, because the costs of such drilling are too great; it is not worth while; it is not desirable from many points of view. I want to go in the direction I have indicated; I may not be able to go far, but that is the direction in which I want to go. I have expressed my personal view, and I do not speak for India.

The Chairman: I should like to thank Mr. Nehru

for the way in which he has dealt with all the questions that have been put to him, and to assure him of our deep interest and gratitude. I hope he will go back to India with the knowledge that there are some people in this country who really do desire not merely to be sympathetic towards India—that is very easy—but to understand the tremendous problems of that great country. We shall watch with interest the events that take place when Mr. Nehru goes back to India, and when he takes up the formidable position of President of the Congress.

A NOTE ON THE LAND PROBLEM *

Any radical change in the land system, involving large-scale co-operative and collectivist farming, must be preceded or accompanied by the ending of the present zamindari or landlord system wherever it prevails. The question arises as to whether compensation should be given to the landlords so dispossessed. If the change can be brought about by peaceful and democratic methods, it would be desirable to give some compensation and so avoid a conflict which is likely to be wasteful and more costly than the compensation itself. But it must be borne in mind that anything in the nature of full compensation is utterly out of the question, especially in so far as the big landlords are concerned. To give such compensation in the shape of bonds would be to mortgage the future of the land

* When Mr. Nehru revised the verbatim report of this meeting he added these paragraphs.

and to continue almost the same burden on the peasantry, though in another form. Therefore a form of compensation would have to be devised which removed this burden and at the same time lessened the distress and upsetting which a change-over would bring to the landlord group. Probably the compensation would be proportionately less higher up in the scale—the middle landlords getting proportionately more than the bigger ones.

It should be remembered that the word "landlord" is rather a misleading one. In the United Provinces (a zamindari province) there are a million and a half so-called landlords. Probably about 85 per cent of them are no better than the tenant class, and many are worse off than the better-off tenants. There can be no question of depriving them of anything; they stand in need of further help and of a reduction of their burdens—debt, revenue, etc. Of the remaining 15 per cent, only a tiny fraction of 1 per cent are really biggish landlords—about 5,000 in all—and about 1,000 of these might be considered the big landlords whose incomes from land vary from about Rs. 12,000 to Rs. 5,000,000 per annum. Those whose incomes run into millions are a mere handful, of course.

During the recent depression and fall in agricultural prices the position of the landlord has steadily deteriorated, and many of the middle landlords are on the verge of bankruptcy. The moneylender holds them, as well as the tenants, in his grip. Some recent legislation has slightly eased the position *vis-à-vis* the moneylender, but it does not go nearly far enough.

Apart from the landlord and the tenant there are large numbers of the landless proletariat who are largely unemployed, or only partially employed during harvesting and other seasons.

The problem in those parts of India where the zamindari system does not prevail (Punjab, Gujerat, South India) and there is peasant proprietorship, is somewhat different. These peasant proprietors are much better off than the tenants of the zamindari areas, but latterly they have also deteriorated greatly. Behind them again are the landless classes, many of these being the so-called depressed classes.

Questions of compensation and the like arise only when an attempt is made, as it should be made, to have a peaceful change-over from one system to another. In the event of upheavals, brought on by delay in making the necessary changes in time, it is impossible to say how matters will shape themselves.